"This is what is written:
The Messiah will suffer and rise from the dead on the
third day, and repentance for the forgiveness of sins
will be preached in his name to all nations,
beginning at Jerusalem."

Luke 24:46–47

"Expect great things from God;
attempt great things for God."
–William Carey

EVOLVING MISSIONS

24 Voices Reflecting on Missions Today

Compiled by

Peter Bunton and Hillary Vargas

House to House Publications
Lititz, PA USA

Evolving Missions
24 Voices Reflecting on Missions Today
Compiled by Peter Bunton and Hillary Vargas

© 2020 DOVE Mission International

ISBN 13: 978-1-7357388-1-9

Published by
House to House Publications
11 Toll Gate Road
Lititz, Pennsylvania 17543 USA
Tele: 800-848-5892
www.h2hp.com

Printed in the United States of America

DEDICATION

This work is dedicated to our God who loves all peoples
and desires all to know Him.

It is also dedicated to our friends, who have left their home
countries and regions, compelled by that same love.

ACKNOWLEDGEMENTS

Our thanks go to those who have made this book possible, from the many contributors who have submitted articles, to those who have edited and proofread. Our particular thanks go to Nancy Leatherman for her hours of proofreading and helpful suggestions which have improved this work. Our gratitude is expressed to Ron Myer, director of DOVE USA, for his tireless support of the work of DOVE Mission International. We also thank Sarah Sauder of House to House Publications for believing in missions and helping steer this book through the rigorous publishing processes.

Dr. Peter Bunton, PhD.

Hillary Vargas

DOVE Mission International

CONTENTS

Introduction 11

1. God Heals, Not the Missionary
   Dave Smith 13

2. Missions Ain't What it Used to Be
   Peter Bunton 16

3. From Heaven to Earth
   Diane Omondi 19

4. Missionary Communication:
   Cultural Awareness and Humility
   Hillary Vargas 26

5. The God Who Speaks Every Language:
   The Ongoing Need for Bible Translation
   Katrina 30

6. Missions: Women in Partnership with Women
   Nancy Shirk 35

7. Commission x 5 = Missions
   Peter Bunton 38

8. Prayer and Worship Leading to Effective Missions
   Dave Smith 41

9. The Challenges and Benefits of Being a Missionary Kid
   W, worker in a creative access nation 45

10. Paying the Price of Cross-Cultural Missions
    Ibrahim Omondi 51

11. A Bridge for the Gospel: Starting Small Businesses
    Dirk Develing 56

12. Open Heart, Open Home
    Nancy Leatherman 59

13. **Medical Missions: From Dispensing Expertise to Collaborative Partnership**
   Dr. T. Scott Jackson, M.D..62

14. **Meeting Jesus through a Social Media Ad: Using Today's Technologies**
   R & M, workers in a creative access nation 65

15. **Chopsticks vs. Forks**
   Wes Dudley..68

16. **Children as Missionaries**
   Josie Wilson 71

17. **Can Evangelism and Social Justice Get Along?**
   Justin Shrum..75

18. **Youth Missions: Coming Back Changed**
   Stephanie Sauder...81

19. **The Unexpected Rewards of Lovingly Serving Others**
   Lynn Ironside 85

20. **Teachers as Students: Education in a Cross-Cultural Setting**
   Gene Stevenson..90

21. **A Widow Multiplying Young Missionaries**
   Nancy Leatherman 96

22. **Missions in a Polluted World**
   Peter Bunton..99

23. **Giving What We Cannot Keep to Gain What We Cannot Lose**
   Nancy Barnett 103

24. **Wide-Eyed Wonder and Raw Humanity: God's Love for Those with Special Needs**
   Elizabeth Vanderhorst...106

25. **Starting a Business in a Creative Access Nation**
R & M, workers in a creative access nation 112

26. **Reaching Unchurched Youth in South Africa**
Joel Smucker 115

27. **A Mission of Making Peace in a
Conflict-Ridden World**
Kellie Swope 119

28. **Missions: Fulfilling the Father's Dreams and Desires**
Bill Landis 124

29. **Reconciliation between Peoples and Nations**
Dave Smith 127

30. **Rest: A Key to Fulfilling the Great Commission**
Shannon Graybill 134

31. **Discovering Family Missions**
Wes Dudley 137

Afterword 140

INTRODUCTION

Welcome to *Evolving Missions: 24 Voices Reflecting on Missions Today!*

So, what is this book about? The idea germinated and began to come to fruition during the summer of 2020, which was a time when world travel almost ceased due to the COVID-19 pandemic. Many missionaries stayed in location and sought new ways to serve the local people. Some of us were finding new ways to support missionaries around the world during this unusual time. We knew that God's desire to bless the nations held true. We were aware that God's mandate to make disciples of the nations still applied, even in the midst of temporary travel setbacks. So, we prayed for nations and missionaries; we raised resources for Jesus' love still to be proclaimed in the nations. . .and somehow, we began to write!

Who are we? Do we feel we are especially equipped to do this? Not really. We are simply a bunch of people, twenty-four of us, who love to follow God's promoting to bless the nations. Some of us have lived in countries other than our own. Others have ongoing commitments to serve specific nations. While not all living overseas, we pray, give, and often visit to support local people and missionaries in their faithful witness to Christ.

This collection of writings comes from a group who are diverse in many ways. We are college students, missionaries, business people, homemakers, therapists, photographers, and web designers. We are in our twenties, sixties, and all ages in between! Some are experienced writers in academia, while others have never written something like this before! As many of us come from a largely homogenous society in rural Lancaster County, Pennsylvania, we admit that we are not the most diverse group in terms of ethnicity and race. Yet, having said that, we do represent at least five nationalities. And between us we have lived in Kenya,

Taiwan, Greece, Germany, Guatemala, Moldova, the United Kingdom, South Africa, New Zealand, Jamaica, Canada, Barbados, the USA, the Netherlands, Grenada, Uganda, Nepal, Belize, and some "creative access" nations. So we have been around a bit!

This book is a set of reflections on world missions. Some articles reflect on the Scriptures or provide a theological framework. Some are about practical strategies in missions today. There are personal testimonies about how God changes us as we follow Him in missions. Many aspects of missions are highlighted, such as missions and children, women, reconciliation, social justice, special needs, prayer, culture, business as mission, the use of technology in missions, suffering, and hospitality, to name only some of the topics found in this book. We trust you will find them informative and be open to see new ways you might engage in God's work around the world today. These thirty-one reflections may be read one per day for a month, or be used as short readings in small groups and prayer groups to help us grow in missiological understanding and the call both to pray and work. There is flexibility—so you decide.

Above all, may God shape you as you read. May He show us all how we can serve Him in our generation so that He is indeed glorified in the nations of the world.

Sincerely,

Dr. Peter Bunton, PhD.
Director, DOVE Mission International

1

God Heals,
Not the Missionary

Dave Smith

I was 18. I had just left everything I'd known and left my home to do a Discipleship Training School with the international organization Youth With A Mission. As part of the school we had a two-month-long cross-cultural outreach in the Pacific Islands. My team of eleven young women and three guys went to the small island nation of Vanuatu. Although it was a beautiful, picturesque group of islands, it was mired in poverty.

Everywhere we went the local people asked us to pray for them, especially for healing. This was a problem for me. I'd grown up in a conservative denomination, and while I believed healing existed, I was sure I couldn't do it. One night in a small, palm frond–covered church the locals once again asked us to pray for healing. The women on the team were super enthusiastic. They began to pray, and witnessed God start to bring healing. What was my response? I hid behind the young women trying not to make contact with anyone. However, a man with a severe arm deformity found me and through the interpreter asked me to pray for him. Full of anxiety, I did the only thing I could think of. I thought of all the televangelists I had seen and shouted, "In the name of Jesus, be healed!" I opened my eyes to see that nothing had changed with this man's arm. Feeling defeated and weak, I went back to the village where we were staying and had a restless night.

The following morning we learned that the same church wanted us to visit again. Everything inside me was praying, "Please don't let that man come back again! I'll be humiliated." Of course, he came! He saw me right away. With a huge smile on his face, he made a beeline for me. He was speaking frantically in the Bislama language, shaking my hand vigorously. Then he turned away and left. I was dumbfounded. Our interpreter then came over and excitedly said, "Did he tell you?"

"I think so, but I don't speak Bislama," I answered.

Responding to my confusion, she began to tell me a story that would shape the rest of my life. That man that I had prayed for went back to his house that night. During his sleep he had a dream that I was praying for him again, but this time God was there as well. When he woke up, his arm was completely healed. He could once again hug his family properly. He could work to provide for his family again. He could lift both arms in adoration of his Father.

In my weakness and unbelief I had completely missed the fact that the hand he had used to shake mine was the one that previously had been deformed. God in his goodness and graciousness healed this man's arm and etched in my heart the beauty of my weakness.

God knows we don't have what it takes. What he asks is for a heart after His own and a raised hand that's willing to go. Since that time, I've seen God heal others through me, but I've known that it's not about me having what it takes to do a miracle. It's about being willing to go to those who need one.

About Dave Smith

Dave has served as a missionary in the South Pacific and Asia for nearly 10 years. During this time he's shared the love of Jesus in Australia, New Zealand, Vanuatu, Fiji, Singapore, Malaysia, Thailand, South Korea, Japan, Germany, and Mexico. David's passion is to lead intimate worship like his biblical namesake and to teach others about the love God has for each one of us. He lives with his wife, Alissa, and their three children in Tauranga, New Zealand.

2

Missions Ain't What it Used to Be

Peter Bunton

"Missions" is a term the church uses frequently. We immediately start to think of remote places in the world and activities such as communicating the Christian gospel to those who have never heard, or educating children in remote villages. The reality is, however, that missions today involves multiple tasks and locations.

The word "missions" comes from the Latin word *missio*, itself from the verb *mittere*, which means "to send." So, technically, the word implies the church sending people on a task. Because "send" implies movement and travel, it has usually been attached to moving from one people or nation to another.

Multiple ways to be a missionary

Today, being sent to communicate the love of Christ can involve multiple media. It could be that we speak and preach to people, but God often uses things such as drama, music, and dance to communicate His love. Moreover, such communication these days may be through websites and social media. Furthermore, the church has always "preached" the gospel through acts of kindness and compassion. Traditionally, one way has been through medical ministry. However, today missions can include feeding programs, or helping people develop a business so that their ongoing needs can be met. Whether you are a teacher, nurse, IT specialist, builder, or mechanic, there is a role for you in the church's task of proclaiming Christ, discipling believers, and seeing new churches started around the world.

Not just one people, but missions to many people at the same time

A further complexity in today's world might mean that a missionary goes to another country to find they are ministering to multiple people groups. For example, American missionaries Justin and Rawan Shrum lead The Justice Project in Germany. As they minister to women caught in human trafficking and exploited in the sex industry, they find they rarely minister to Germans, but to Russians, Bulgarians, Colombians, and Nigerians. While called to Germany as their context for ministry, their outreach is to diverse peoples within that context.

Cross-cultural missions at home

Today, missions might also mean staying in your home community, but reaching those of other cultural and linguistic groups. Most countries have large immigrant populations, many of which are not Christian. Indeed, they may be active adherents to another religion such as Islam or Buddhism. If we only think of missions as traveling somewhere on a plane, we may miss the multiple people groups near our home who also have never heard the gospel of Jesus Christ. Especially as they are in a new country and culture, they are often open to new relationships and ways of thinking, and can be the very ripe harvest field of which Jesus spoke (John 4:35).

Foreign and indigenous missionaries working together

For some, missions can mean not even serving immigrants, but strategically helping those indigenous in your country, but who are from different tribes and religions. This is the case for a number of DOVE Africa missionaries who remain in their home country, yet serve those of other tribes, many of whom are Muslim.

The power of their witness is enhanced through providing quality education or medical services to those who otherwise would be marginalized. An interesting dynamic in these situations is that foreigners support this mission through financial giving, but also through visiting teams. Such short-term foreign teams, while engaging in international missions, are doing so in the spirit of serving the long-term vision of the indigenous missionaries.

There are many ways to engage in missions today. Some may still need to fly to another country, but others of us may find a rich cross-cultural mission field closer to home. May God help each one of us know how we can engage in God's missionary task today.

About Peter Bunton

Peter, originally from Great Britain, lives in Pennsylvania. His main responsibility is the director of DOVE Mission International, where he helps develop and send missionaries from the USA. He received a PhD in missiology from the University of Manchester, England, for his research in founders' succession in international Christian movements and organizations.

3

From Heaven to Earth

Diane Omondi

Jesus walked on this earth for thirty-three years. Only the final three of those were focused on public ministry. Can you imagine, with me, Jesus' homecoming back into heaven? Of course, He was welcomed with open arms by His heavenly Father. As He took His place at the right hand of the throne, perhaps He and His Father had a conversation.

"So, how did it go, Jesus?" the Father might have asked.

"It was really good, my Father," replied Jesus. "I healed the sick. I cast out demons. I preached in all the towns of Galilee."

"That's great, my Son," God could have replied. "But what about the rest of the world?"

"Oh, I finished my work. I left the rest to my disciples."

Really? Did Jesus entrust the rest of the world to His twelve disciples and, by extension, to us?

Yes, He did. The question that follows is obvious. How are we doing? Have we finished the task?

It is encouraging to know that Christianity is gaining ground, so to speak, around the world. But before we rejoice too rigorously, we need to understand that statistic in the context of world population growth. Pew Research Center[1] projects that over the next three decades, if current trends continue, Christians will remain the largest religious group but Islam will grow at a faster rate than any other major religion. By 2050, again based on current trends, the number of Muslims will nearly equal the number of Christians around the world. If the trends continue, it is projected that Islam could be the largest religion by 2070.

According to Joshua Project,[2] there are 7,300 least-reached people groups in the world, making up over 40% of the world's population. Those are not just people who are not born-again Christians. Rather, those are people who have never heard an effective and authentic message of the story of Jesus Christ, His love, and salvation.

In order to interpret this information, it is important to give some basic definitions. An unreached people group (UPG) is a group that does not have enough followers of Christ among them to evangelize their own people. A least-reached people group (LRPG) is one in which less than 2% are evangelical Christians in any given country. Missions, in the context we are using, is sharing the love of Christ in a different culture. It is a specialized type of evangelism. Yes, we all need to share God's love with our neighbors, family, friends, workmates, communities. But we also need to share the gospel outside of our "Jerusalem." If we do not, the world will simply never be reached.

Based on all this, I don't think we have finished the task Jesus left for us. I pray that the projected trends will be turned around, and I believe they will. But it will require both divine and human intervention. Apart from praying for God to sovereignly move, what can we do about it?

Call and command

As much as God's calling to missions is necessary and important, the term "call" can easily be misunderstood. Missions is not only related to call. It is also related to command. In other words, we are not entitled to just sit and wait until we "feel" called. The command is clear. We all need to be involved in missions.

We tend to think that a certain select few among us are given this "call." Not so. We probably know the Great Commission Jesus gave His disciples before going up to heaven (Matthew 28:19–20). Does that commission not mention "all nations?" The word translated as "nations" is the word *ethne* in Greek, which would more accurately be translated "races," "tribes," or "ethnic groups." These are the groups mentioned above as being 7,300 still unreached.

We often interpret the Great Commission as a call to evangelism and discipleship. Very true. But even if every single believer were to reach his or her *oikos* (literally "house," but often used to refer to one's network of relationships) and his or her neighborhood with the gospel, we will still not be able to reach all *ethne*. In order to finish this task, cross-cultural missions is required. We need people who will move—physically, linguistically, and culturally—into a nation or community that is not his or her own. We must cross over! Apart from divine visitations from Jesus through the power of the Holy Spirit, there is no other way to complete the task.

More than Bible teachers

An appeal for missionaries found in a missions magazine recently reads something like this. *Needed: academicians, accountants, administrators, computer technicians, automotive technicians, teachers, web developers, writers, counselors, English teachers, engineers, doctors, nurses, social workers, financial managers, businessmen.*

You might be saying, "What? I am going to share the gospel of Jesus Christ, not to advance my profession!" The fact is, you can and should do both.

We once visited a missionary couple sent into an Islamic community by a different ministry here in Kenya. We arrived at their home midday. They were in the house, studying the Bible. Studying the Bible is a good thing to do, by the way.

"How is it going here?" we asked.

"Things are very hard," they answered. "These people don't accept us. They don't even know English. We have only found a few people we can even talk to."

"What are you doing to build relationships?" we asked.

"We have invited them to come for Bible study in our home, but they are not interested." (Remember, this is an Islamic community.) "Some of them are even hostile and are accusing us of trying to take them out of their religion."

Well, that is exactly what you are doing, I was thinking, but did not say. The discussion continued.

"These people are so dirty," was one comment. "We can't get any decent food supplies here," another complained. "It is really boring to stay in the house all day."

As far as we could tell, they had no respect for the community, no vision for providing a social service, and no plan for learning the language.

It was disappointing, but not surprising, when we heard six months later that the mission station had closed.

Meanwhile, several miles away, DOVE missionaries are thriving. One is now a village elder in an Islamic community. Another is on the local agriculture committee and is involved in discussions about how to improve farming in the village. Another is a highly respected teacher who is sought out by many parents for tuition, advice, and prayer. (Yes, prayer.) Others are called into homes for medical emergencies. Another is often contacted by community leaders to pray when things are not going well in the village. The list could go on. In all these, there are ripe opportunities for showing love, being a friend, and sharing the gospel.

We're talking long-term

The ultimate goal when reaching a LRPG is to see that particular group come out of the LRPG category and become a *reached* people group. For example, the DOVE Missions Africa (DMA) vision statement is "to see least-reached people groups knowing and accepting the saving power of Jesus Christ and making Him known." Our mission is to impact least-reached people groups with the gospel through evangelism, discipleship, ministry to human needs, and indigenous, reproducing churches.

The phrase "indigenous, reproducing churches" highlights that we desire to reach the place where believers in Christ within that people group have the capacity to evangelize their own people and establish reproducing churches. When that happens, the missionary's job is over. It is time to leave. But we need to recognize that it could take many years, decades, or maybe even a lifetime to reach that goal.

When God calls us to reach a people group, we need to think of more than a six-month or even two-year commitment.

Cultural integrity

It is said that every culture is integral to itself. That is, within its own context, any given culture makes sense. There's a reason why one assumes that a more well-to-do brother will pay school fees for my children. There's a reason why a pastor wears a suit and tie on Sunday, even in sweltering heat. Even though you might not agree with the practice, it still stands that if you grew up in that culture and situation, you would probably do the same. You would not "know better."

A missionary who is reaching a "new" people group must be ready to integrate. Accept. Identify. Appreciate. In that process, language learning is an essential first step to any long-term cross-cultural assignment. We are not saying a missionary has to (for example) start walking around naked if that is the cultural practice. But respect and understanding are crucial.

We do not go to the mission field to "fix" other people. We do not go to prove them wrong. Jesus came all the way from heaven to earth—how is that for crossing cultures? He learned our trades, ate our food, became our friend, and in the process, challenged us to walk on a higher path.

It takes everyone

Many people respond to this type of discussion by saying, "I am not called to missions." Fair enough. Clearly, not everyone in the church can leave home and go to a foreign land. Who would send funds? Who would stay home and pray? Who would visit the missionary?

Let's go back, however, to the thought that missions is a matter of command, not only call. If that is true, then every believer is commanded to be involved in some way. It might not be going. It might be giving. It might be praying. It might be visiting. Whatever the area of involvement, we are all called (that is, all commanded) to pursue those who are not reached so as to share God's love and salvation.

Eternity is waiting

"And this gospel of the kingdom will be preached in the whole world as a testimony to *all nations, and then* the end will come" (Matthew 24:14; emphasis mine).

Sure enough, here comes our word *ethne* again. Once all tribes and races have heard the gospel, it seems we also, like Jesus, will have finished our work. The time will then be right for Jesus' return.

May we love like Jesus, sacrifice like Jesus, and influence like Jesus to see all *ethne* reached. He gave us that task. We need to finish it so He can come back for His bride.

1. https://www.pewforum.org/2019/10/17/in-u-s-decline-of-christianity-continues-at-rapid-pace/
2. https://joshuaproject.net/people_groups/statistics

About Diane Omondi

Diane sensed a clear call to a life of cross-cultural missions while a student at Goshen College, Indiana, in the late 70s. A term abroad in Costa Rica, getting to know Ibrahim Omondi in their student campus fellowship, and a visit to Kenya in 1980 all served to confirm and clarify that call. After getting married in 1983, Ibrahim and Diane have been serving in Kenya. Diane leads DOVE Missions Africa, through which many have been sent to serve among least-reached people groups in Kenya and other East African nations.

4

Missionary Communication: Cultural Awareness and Humility

Hillary Vargas

In a small Moldovan town, there is a church that I attended for a few months. The pastor's wife was the worship director. The songs she chose were usually songs that I was familiar with, except we were singing in Romanian and Russian. The songs were pre-recorded with minimal instruments, but still had a very Western feel. I noticed that while the Moldovan church members sang the songs and knew them well, they wouldn't respond to the music by clapping or raising their hands.

One day, the worship leader decided to sing a song that had a very Moldovan/Eastern European feel to it. This was the first time I had heard this type of music within the church walls. At first I didn't notice any reaction from the church members, but then I noticed a man who was tapping his foot to the beat. I was surprised at first, but it actually made sense. The people hadn't been singing songs from their culture at this church; they had been singing translated versions of another culture's music that they couldn't really connect to. Translating the song wasn't enough; the song itself needed to be from Moldova in order for the people to respond from their hearts.

I wonder how differently these church members would worship if they sang songs that were made in the traditional Moldovan style. At weddings and parties, these fast-paced, upbeat songs are played at full volume, and the people dance with high energy while shouting from the top of their lungs, with light practically shining from their faces. To see this is to see true freedom in self-expression. I can only imagine how the worship services would be if there existed songs of this type with worship lyrics.

When we do any sort of outreach, whether in another culture or in a subculture of our own, how do we think about the people we are trying to reach? What music do they relate to? What part of their culture must we understand in order to communicate God's love in the most effective way? How can we reach the people from within their culture rather than reaching out from our own? Jesus did this whenever he told a parable. His disciples and the communities He visited were largely made up of farmers, so in order to reach their hearts, he first reached their minds through the common understanding of agriculture. He told stories like the shepherd leaving his herd to go find one sheep that was lost (Luke 15:3–7); He used the analogy of Jesus being the vine and believers being the fruit-bearing branches that grow from the vine (John 15:1–17); He even caused an actual fig tree to wither as an illustration of how our faith should stand (Mark 11:12–14, 20–26). If Jesus were conducting his earthly ministry today, I can imagine that in order to reach us, He would tell quite a few parables using cat memes and referencing modern technology. (Something akin to "I am the power strip, and you are the charging cord. Anyone who remains plugged into me will always produce a phone with a fully charged battery.")

How can we reach the minds of those we serve in order to ultimately reach their hearts with the gospel message?

Assuming that I know nothing

One key to reaching people is through humility. If we enter a new culture thinking that a) we already know how to do a certain thing and b) that how we do it is the only way to do it, that automatically creates a barrier between us and anyone we may be trying to serve. This next story illustrates how *not* to do this.

Lessons from Moldovan ham

In Moldova, the town I lived in had a nice downtown area with shops and a couple of restaurants. There was also a deli chain that had a few locations around the country. I had bought a few things there before, and never thought of it as being any different from ordering from a deli in my local grocery store in Pennsylvania. But one particular day, I decided to order some lunch meat for sandwiches. I ordered 500 grams of the ham and perused the other deli options while the attendant prepared the meat. She handed me the bag of ham, and when I looked at it, I noticed that I was holding one chunk of ham, not the sliced ham I had assumed I was ordering. I asked her, "Why is this not sliced?" She replied simply, "You didn't ask me to slice it." My pride flared as I thought to myself, *I shouldn't have to ask you to slice it. This is a* deli, *for crying out loud*! I asked her if she could slice the piece she had just given to me, but she said that it was too small to be cut on the machine. No thinly sliced meat for me that day!

Instead of internally responding with pride, what if I had thought about what made more sense culturally? Something like, *Oh, that actually makes sense. I've more often seen people chop up blocks of ham for traditional salads than I've ever seen people eat sandwiches. In fact, I've never seen anyone eat a sandwich with sliced meat in the year and a half that I've lived here.* Having this type of response automatically come to mind may require a paradigm shift of seeing other cultures through their own lens rather than through our own. Assuming that I knew nothing about how to order at a deli could have prevented that small wall from being built up inside me as a result of that experience.

Changing our paradigm

This paradigm shift can be applied in missions as well. Just because evangelicals in the USA worship with guitars and drums doesn't mean that we should take guitars and drums to the mountains of Peru or to the Indian countryside and expect the people to suddenly worship God "appropriately." In fact, the very way in which we present the gospel could potentially build a wall between us and someone from another culture, as illustrated below.

Could it be that when we take the "American" way of doing things with us in missions (which we *will* if we don't think about it beforehand), the people we are trying to reach might not respond well to our way of communicating, our way of building trust, or our way of presenting the gospel story?[1] For example, think about how a person with a Western background might present the gospel message to a room full of people versus someone of an Asian background. A Westerner would likely first present the fact that Jesus loves us and died for our sins, followed by explaining why. An Asian would most likely start in Genesis and tell the backstory of the Jews before arriving at Jesus' ministry, death, and resurrection.[2] If you as a Westerner presented the facts first to someone in Asia, they may wonder if you think they are stupid enough to just take a "fact" at face value without first showing them the bigger picture, followed by how all of the pieces fit together. Likewise, if you as someone with an Asian cultural background start in Genesis when presenting the gospel to Westerners, you run the risk of losing the attention of your audience fairly quickly.

Being aware of the culture we enter on the mission field, and responding to everything with humility helps us to reach people's minds and then their hearts, the way Jesus would have.

1. The book *The Culture Map*, by Erin Meyer, (2015) dissects several actions that we take in cross-cultural situations and offers a continuum for each one. Cultures can be placed anywhere along each continuum. Communicating, trusting, and persuading are three of these continua.
2. *The Culture Map*, pp.104–112.

About Hillary Vargas

Hillary has joined and co-led short-term teams to Guatemala. After serving as a Peace Corps volunteer in the Republic of Moldova from 2014 to 2016 with her husband, Adrin, Hillary has felt her long-term call to missions through administration. She has worked in the DMI office in Lititz, PA, since 2018.

5

The God Who Speaks Every Language

The Ongoing Need for Bible Translation

Katrina

"The story of missions the whole world over shows that
the success or failure of missions has always been
dependent on whether those brought to Christ have
the Scriptures in their own language or not."

–G. Campbell Morgan

Translating the Bible into each Himalayan language

Imagine seeing a miracle before your very eyes and having no
way of getting to know the one who performed it. Imagine giving
yourself to a new walk of faith yet having no manual to help you
on your way. This is a familiar story for many of the people we
meet on our travels.

Over the last three years my husband, Dan, and I have lived
in the Himalayas. We have given ourselves to learning the language
of the nation we now call home. Our hope is to be able to build
long-lasting friendships. We desire to see the nation discipled in
a way that doesn't nullify the importance of their own tongue. We
are dedicating time to seeing the Bible translated into every language of the region. Many workers have gone before us translating
the obscure languages of the Himalayas. We rejoice that only 24

out of 123 languages remain "unengaged" and without Scripture.

In one nation where we have lived, there are 170 people groups and over 120 languages. It's only been about 70 years since there were an estimated 100 believers in the entire nation. Today that number has reached well over one million. There is no denying a powerful move of God in this land!

A common idea among local nonbelievers is that Christianity is a Western religion. Our desire is to see the native people worship the Lord in their own unique expression of worship, whether that be with native instruments, dances, or poetry. We want accurately to represent Jesus as the one who speaks every language. He's not a distant or foreign god who cannot hear and cannot speak. Instead He wants to step beyond the barriers of language to make His home in the hearts of anyone who calls on Him.

Back in 2014, before I began my journey into missions, God showed me a picture of the earth. I could see people belonging to every tribe, tongue, and people group. They began to lift their faces and arms heavenwards. In that moment I felt God's aching heart for every person to see Him and know Him in all His glory and His desire that they would be free to worship Him in their own unique way. I believe this was a moment that marked me for long-term missions.

Encountering people's desperate need for God and His Word

In March 2018, I was just a few weeks pregnant with our first child. I took a trip with a team to one of the more mountainous regions in the country. The goal of our time there was to "scout" the area, praying and asking the Lord for people of peace and open doors. One of our teammates, Sharon,[1] wrote an account of one particular encounter.

"As we were walking through part of the valley, a lady came up beside us being friendly and inquisitive. Shortly after, our teammate Stephanie[1] began to share the Kingdom message. She was confronted with a strong rebuke! The woman told her to be quiet.

We would be in serious trouble if the Lamas (Buddhist teachers) found out what we were talking about. This was a clear warning for us to talk with caution. We prayed over Stephanie, who was visibly shaken and trembling with fear. Peace overcame and we were able to continue our journey."

One year later, during a trip back to the same region, Pam[1] told us this story, showing that God clearly had not finished with this family!

"After walking for about nine hours, I began to feel fatigued. I told my daughter that I could not go on and had to stop. I was too tired. Oddly for me, this was the first time I had felt like this. I am usually one of the last people in the group to be complaining of exhaustion. Back in the day, I used to be an Olympic cross-country skier. But here I met my limit. I told my daughter that if we could find a place to stay near the path, we would have to stop.

"Just around the corner was a house. We stopped and prayed and asked the Lord if it would be possible for us to stay here the night. I suddenly realized this was the same house where Stephanie had had the nasty shock of being warned not to come here with the gospel message.

"As we approached, we were kindly invited in and spent some time conversing with the family. Remembering the warning we had received last year, we kept the conversation light.

"Suddenly, the mother of the family asked if we were followers of Jesus. This was amazing! I replied that we were. I also explained that we were only there on holiday. The mother then asked if I would pray for her baby son, who was sick. I entered into their cultural way. I asked, 'Have you not taken the baby to the Buddhist monk to perform the necessary rights and mantras?' The mother said that she had not. I added that as a follower of Jesus if my child got sick, I would pray to Jesus for healing. She asked me again if I could pray for her son in Jesus' name.

"The mother would not stop talking about Jesus. Then I turned to the grandfather and asked him why they were so interested in Jesus. What he said next was something that I had been praying for and dreaming to hear for years. He said, 'From what I have heard about Jesus, He shows us the true way of life. We want to follow Him.' He continued on to say, 'I cannot read, so how can I guide my family? Will you please be our guide?'

"This was a special moment for me. My heart was being ripped apart, as I knew we could not stay long. I would need to leave the country due to restrictions of visas and permits and politics. There were so many barriers just to get here. On top of that, finding a way to stay and be a guide is so often beyond our imagination. But the Holy Spirit is at work and is the ultimate guide. We prayed for the baby and blessed him.

"I passed on some newly translated Bible stories for them to listen to. I instructed them simply to listen. We told them to talk to Jesus using His name and to trust themselves to Him. I encouraged them that the Father had heard their cry for help and not to give up."

This story demonstrates why we long to see the Scriptures translated. There are people out there who are hungry. They are waiting to receive the precious Word of God for the very first time.

The spoken Word of God

Currently, we have been taking steps to see portions of Scripture translated so that every person would have the Scripture in their mother tongue. The language we are focusing on is unique and very different from the national language. One of our steps towards our goal includes attending an oral Bible translation seminar. At that seminar we learned how to create audio clips of Scripture. This is a much more effective discipleship tool in an area which is largely illiterate. We have also made connections with some key people in our area. These people have already been working among this people group. We have been learning from them how best to approach the task. Lastly, we have committed to taking trips to a particular northern region of the country. We will return there as often as visas (and viruses!) allow.

There will be a day when God will receive a day and night worship from these remote tribes of the Himalayas. Right now He's drawing hearts to Himself and working in ways we cannot even ask for or imagine. As we continue serving, we long to see the 24 remaining languages reduced to zero; then every spoken language in this nation would have access to the Word of God.

1. Not their real names.

About Katrina

Katrina and her husband, Dan, have since 2017 lived in the Himalayas with a ministry predominantly focused on prayer and worship. This couple also have a passion for Bible translation, desiring to see the Scriptures in every language of the Himalayan peoples.

6

Missions: Women in Partnership with Women

Nancy Shirk

In January 2020, seven women of all age groups and from different churches embarked on a two-week missions trip to Kadawa in western Kenya. Some of us had never met each other before we gathered at the airport for departure.

Our goal was to work with Hesbone and Violet Odindo, leaders of DOVE International in Kenya, based in the city of Kisumu. Hesbone and Violet are from the village of Kadawa, not far from Kisumu. This had been a place of great poverty and sickness in the past, as it was largely an area of swamplands. Under the Odindos' leadership, God has enabled the land to become a fertile place of fruit growing. A well has been bored to provide water for irrigation and to meet the needs of the local community. Restoration Community Church, which has thrived in the region, began and Victory Christian School was founded to educate the people of the village and surrounding area.

Before leaving the USA for Kenya, our priority was to have a team back home praying for us. We then worked to raise money from local businesses and friends to buy new shoes for the children at Victory Christian School. We also had friends and family members help us sew washable sanitary pads for the women. We packed our extra suitcases with underwear, pads, clothing, bags, and a sewing machine.

Our first project was to meet with the teenage girls at Victory Christian School. We gave them a small bag with new underwear and sanitary pads. Giving sanitary items might seem strange to some, but in Kadawa, many girls miss school because they do not have proper sanitary supplies. Violet explained to the young women how to use and care for the sanitary supplies, then we prayed a blessing over each girl.

We helped fit 500 children with their new shoes or outfits. The kids that didn't need new shoes received a new outfit. Violet had pre-ordered all of the clothing from a local business. The children danced with delight as they put on their shoes and clothes.

We journeyed through the bush to visit thirty widows who attend Restoration Community Church. We could feel the presence of the Holy Spirit as we sang worship songs while we walked. As the women told us their stories, we cried, laughed, and prayed with them. We also were able to distribute food supplied through Restoration Community Church's ministry to those widows who may have lost their income when they lost their husbands.

Inter-cultural fellowship

While in Kenya, we were able to enjoy a women's retreat on the shores of Lake Victoria. The women's director from the church made the arrangements for the women to ride a bus to a small game park in nearby Kisumu. When the bus entered the park, the women sang worship songs in their language. Some of them had never been that far from home before, or seen the animals that live in their own country. After a boat ride on Lake Victoria, we had a picnic on the ground, worshipped together, and received an inspirational message. It was pure joy to spend time with those beautiful sisters in Christ from a different country and culture.

Sunday morning, at Restoration Community Church, one of the ladies from our team preached an amazing message of encouragement. She felt God was calling her to step out in that way before we went to Kenya. God was stretching us all as we sought to grow in partnership and service of God together with these women.

We, the foreign visitors, received much as we became friends with the local helpers as they told us their heartbreaking stories. We prayed with them for inner healing, and for their families and marriages. They also taught us how to cook some of the local food.

Entrepreneurship

The team brought a sewing machine for the village ministry. Evenings were spent training Violet how to sew. Before we left, she had completed two dresses. She is now designing and sewing her own dresses. This initiative was helping Violet fulfill her dream of starting a sewing center in the village, where the woman can sew uniforms for the school as well as employ local women. School uniforms are mandatory; most of the children, however, can't afford to pay for them. Violet also wants to sew them to sell to other schools in the area in order to raise money for Victory Christian School, thus creating a sustainable business.

One of the prayer times together was precious to us all. The Holy Spirit fell on us and we began praying and prophesying over each other. We were bonded together as sisters in Christ for His Kingdom purposes.

In many parts of the world women are discriminated against and set at a disadvantage. Yet, conversely, it is often the women who raise the family and engage in entrepreneurial activity to provide for the family due to the men often being absent. God loves women and desires them to be change agents in their communities. Supporting them in international partnerships is an essential part of God's heart and mission today.

About Nancy Shirk

Nancy, from Akron, Pennsylvania, has always had a heart for world missions. She has served on mission teams in Canada, Jamaica, and Kenya. She is a member of DOVE Mission International's leadership team and attends DOVE Westgate Church. Nancy is particularly involved in helping ministries in western Kenya.

7

Commission x 5 = Missions

Peter Bunton

Not one commission, but five

In the church we often talk about the Great Commission. In doing so, we usually think of some of the final words of Jesus Christ to His disciples found in Matthew 28:18–20:

"All authority in heaven and on earth has been given to me. Therefore go and make disciples of all nations, baptizing them in the name of the Father and of the Son and of the Holy Spirit, and teaching them to obey everything I have commanded you. And surely I am with you always, to the very end of the age."

The reality is, however, that there are five great commission statements from Jesus. Put together, we understand the missionary task.

The need for disciples

In the commission above, the emphasis is that of making disciples. In fact, in the original Greek, the only verb in the imperative (command form) is the verb "make disciples."

Preach, preach, preach

In the Gospel of Mark (Mark 16:15), we are told, "Go into all the world and preach the gospel to all creation." Here, Jesus seems to emphasize not the goal of making disciples, but the means of achieving it, which is the preaching and communication of the gospel. We are therefore commissioned to communicate, which today can take many forms, including music, drama, art, and social media.

It's all about liberation

A third commission to missions can be found in Luke 24:46–48. Particularly in verse 47, Jesus states that "repentance for the forgiveness of sins will be preached in His name to all nations." Here, Jesus focuses on the content of our preaching, which is to be calling people to turn from sin and receive forgiveness. The word "forgiveness" literally means "untying" and "letting go." We are, therefore, commissioned to bring a message of liberation to all people.

Do it the Jesus way

A fourth commission is found in John 20:21–22. "Again Jesus said: 'Peace be with you! As the Father has sent me, I am sending you.' And with that he breathed on them and said, 'Receive the Holy Spirit. If you forgive anyone his sins, they are forgiven. If you do not forgive them, they are not forgiven.'" Here we are commissioned not to engage in missions in any fashion, but only in the manner in which the Father sent His Son. This speaks to engaging in missions in the very spirit and humility of Christ. In this passage the emphasis seems to be on the manner in which we engage in God's commission.

Holy Spirit power

Lastly, in Acts 1:8, Jesus says, "But you will receive power when the Holy Spirit comes on you; and you will be my witnesses in Jerusalem, and in all Judea and Samaria, and to the ends of the earth." Here we are commissioned to rely on the power and resources of the Holy Spirit and to allow the gifts of the Holy Spirit, such as healing and words of knowledge, to flow through us as we share the love of Christ. Our commission, therefore, is not just to rely on words, but demonstrations of God's power.

Putting it all together

So, we are commissioned multiple times! We are given a goal (making disciples); we are sent to preach and communicate; we are sent to emphasize a turning to Christ to receive freedom; we are encouraged to serve in humility in the very spirit of Christ; and we are given the power and resources to do the commission God gives us. With all these "commissions" flowing together, the church makes a huge difference in transforming the world.

About Peter Bunton

Peter, originally from Great Britain, lives in Pennsylvania. His main responsibility is the director of DOVE Mission International, where he helps develop and send missionaries from the USA. He received a PhD in missiology from the University of Manchester, England, for his research in founders' succession in international Christian movements and organizations.

8

Prayer and Worship Leading to Effective Missions

Dave Smith

Thousands of years ago an insignificant shepherd boy began to worship God with his whole heart. No one was watching. No one was listening. However, when the time came for God to anoint His option for a king over His covenantal people, He deemed David qualified because of his heart. Not because of his skill. Not because he had a master's degree in political science. Not because he was royalty, but because he had a heart that God likened to His own heart.

As David went through the ups and downs of his life, he continued to pray and worship. From 1 Chronicles, we learn that he had a vision for what honoring God in true prayer and worship would look like. When he became king he paid an exorbitant price to set up a new tabernacle that would bring praise to the One who deserves it. He set up his tent and hired 288 singers, 4,000 musicians and 4,000 gatekeepers so that day and night there would always be praises and incense rising up to the throne room of heaven. Biblical scholars estimate the cost for this tabernacle would have equaled $100 billion! No small sum! David recognized the value of giving extravagantly to God and laying down what one has at His feet. Just like Mary of Bethany. Just like the disciples. Just like Jesus.

So what does this have to do with missions? Before Jesus' ascension to heaven, He spoke to His disciples about what we refer to as "the Great Commission." It is often quoted, "Therefore go and make disciples of all nations, baptizing them in the name of the Father, and of the Son and of the Holy Spirit, and teaching them to obey everything I have commanded you" (Matthew 28:19–20). What a clear and powerful statement. Many missionaries quote it and live it out daily. In Acts 1:4–6, moreover, Jesus tells the disciples not to leave, or rather not to leave *yet*! He implores them first to wait for the Holy Spirit so that they would be empowered to bring the name of Jesus to the ends of the earth.

We can't do it in our own strength

I imagine the disciples must have been so confused! "Wait, Jesus, you're telling us to go but not to go until we experience something we've never experienced before?" Jesus in His beautiful wisdom was letting them know that there was no way they could achieve what He was asking in their own power. By staying in prayer, adoration, worship, and obedience, the disciples shifted their hearts to a place where the Holy Spirit could enter and help them in mighty ways. At Pentecost, in one day a dozen fragile and weak men encountered the breath of God and saw 3,000 come to know the name of Jesus right outside the temple that David had dreamed of many years before.

Many times when we feel the touch of God stirring us to go and do missions, we can have a superhero mentality. "Yes, Lord, I will go and save the world!" We may think it even if we don't speak it. Let's get this straight. No one has what it takes without God qualifying us. In fact, many missionaries I know (including myself) will tell you that all they did was raise their hand and say "yes." God did the rest. He qualifies us in those times when no one is looking–in the back hills like David, in our bedrooms in the early hours of the morning, in the prayer meetings where only a few people show up.

It's an amazing thing to be willing to go for Jesus, to have the faith to lay down all that you have to move across the world and minister the love of Jesus to a different culture. Being so far away from home and all that you know can lead to tiredness and burnout. It's the intimacy from cultivating a real heart-level relationship with the Creator of all things that sustains us in those difficult times and spurs us to continue.

Prayer movements

So, how do we see the relationship between prayer, worship, and missions today? In Germany in the eighteenth century, the Moravians were moved to do what David had dreamed of. They began a hundred-year movement of night and day prayer. Over that century, sometimes as few as two or three people kept the dream alive. They did, however, become the first Protestant movement of missionaries, sending lay people into missions, and some of the first to minister to slaves in the Americas. It was a great missions movement, springing from a hundred-year, 24-hour-a-day prayer movement.

According to Debbie Przybylski of Intercessors Arise International, in 1995 there were around twenty-four day and night prayer houses.[1] Today there are 674 Houses of Prayer in North America and many more in other nations including those where Christianity is suppressed.[2] Worship music has also grown at an unprecedented rate. In the last 40 years movements of churches such as Vineyard, Hillsong, and Bethel have written songs of praise sung in many languages and in many remote places. The International House of Prayer (IHOP) in Missouri, USA, has had 20,000 full-time staff in the last 20 years alone.[3] Currently there are fresh movements to establish prayer houses from Asia to Jerusalem along the Silk Road!

I believe we've entered into a time where God has again highlighted the importance of what it means to worship Him in spirit and truth, because such worship helps the people of the earth see Jesus in us. Anyone can tell another that Jesus *exists*. Only someone who has experienced Jesus on a heart level in that secret place can really share with another who Jesus *is*! I don't want to be a superhero, but I do want to lay down my life, all that I have, and allow God to show Himself through me.

1. http://nations-hop.org/the-increase-of-houses-of-prayer-worldwide
2. http://www.ihopnetwork.com/index.php/home/hop-list
3. https://mikebickle.org/watch/2019_08_23_1900_MB_FC

About Dave Smith

Dave has served as a missionary in the South Pacific and Asia for nearly 10 years. During this time he's been privileged to share the love of Jesus in Australia, New Zealand, Vanuatu, Fiji, Singapore, Malaysia, Thailand, South Korea, Japan, Germany, and Mexico. David's passion is to lead intimate worship like his biblical namesake and to teach others about the love God has for each one of us. He lives with his wife, Alissa, and their three children in Tauranga, New Zealand.

9

The Challenges and Benefits of Being a Missionary Kid

W

He must manage his own family well and see that his
children obey him, and he must do so in a manner worthy
of full respect. (If anyone does not know how to manage
his own family, how can he take care of God's church?)

1 Timothy 3:4–5

Sometimes, when our work is the thrilling, urgent, and essential task of bringing the Kingdom of God to those who do not yet know it, it is even more tempting than usual to wrap our very existence around this work. 1 Timothy 3 excludes this idea. Raising a child is of no less importance to the missionary than it is to any other parent. To be sure, every believer is to radically put Jesus before family (Luke 14:26), and He sometimes asks His servants to do things that dramatically affect their children (think of Hosea's kids' names). Jesus makes clear, however, that loving Him includes loving children (Mark 9:37), and the psalmist claims that "out of the mouth of babies and infants you have established strength" (Psalm 8:2, English Standard Version [ESV]). Little children are a big deal in God's eyes, and in no way a secondary calling for the missionary.

So as we discuss the children in missionary families, let's be clear. Every child is incredibly unique, and missionary kids are no exception. Even siblings that go through almost identical experiences may process these in drastically different ways. Yet there are some commonalities that many missionary kids seem to experience. This article, though by no means comprehensive, will try to deal with some of the major ones.

Some terms

Let's go over a couple terms that will be used throughout this article. Missionary kids, or MKs, are individuals whose parents are/were (usually cross-cultural) missionaries during part or all of their developmental years. Since "home country" is a complicated subject for MKs, we will use the term "passport country" to refer to the MK's country of nationality (usually what their parents would consider their home country), and for lack of a better term, we will use "country of service" to describe the country/ies in which an MK's parents are/were serving as missionaries.

Since MKs usually spend their developmental years in more than one country/culture, or at least have major influences from multiple cultures, they often do not fully acculturate or associate with either their passport country or their country of service. Instead, the children develop their own third culture, which is sometimes a blend of the two countries and sometimes includes cultural tendencies not found in either. Because of this phenomenon we refer to them as "third culture kids," or TCKs.

Challenges

Being or raising a TCK has some wonderful benefits, but it also comes with some very real challenges. Perhaps the most common and most obvious is the lack of a sense of belonging. An MK's passport may say their home is one country while they have lived most of their lives in another. This often leads to feeling out of place in either. Their friends may all have similar experiences that the MK hasn't lived through or jokes that the MK doesn't understand. This can be especially difficult when an MK moves to their passport country and expects to fit in, but finds ways in which their childhood, education, worldviews, and even preferences do not line up with all of their would-be peers' preferences. As a grown-up MK myself, I still cringe a little when I enter my passport country and border control says, "Welcome home."

Education

A related challenge that missionaries face with their children is the issue of schooling. Usually a missionary will want their child to receive an education of similar quality as their passport country, which may not always be available in their country of service (not to mention how to deal with religion classes in many of the most unreached countries). Some missionaries homeschool, some send their kids to local schools, some even do both at once! And then there is the infamous MK boarding school option. Some kids thrive in this structure, but others really struggle to see why their parents "don't want them around." Each option has its advantages and disadvantages, and missionaries need a lot of wisdom to decide what is best for each child.

Extended family

The issue of extended family is also a sensitive matter that missionaries must consider for their kids. Modern communication technology has helped in so many ways to keep MKs connected to their extended family, but there's still a difference between a weekly Skype call and dropping the kids off at Grandma's for the day. The fact that an MK is also a TCK whereas perhaps all of their cousins are not can also make it difficult for an MK to feel connected to family.

Does God love MKs?

A final, serious challenge facing many MKs is the idea that God doesn't love them. They may have had to suddenly leave family, friends, and comfort behind without having any say in the matter, which for anyone, child or adult, is traumatic. But for the MK, this happened because of what God wanted. Perhaps God doesn't care about what I want? Perhaps God's will doesn't include my happiness? Sadly, despite the wonderful faith of their parents, some MKs choose to leave the faith, and I would not be surprised if this is the core reason behind most of them. I myself needed a lot of growth as a young adult to understand that God truly loved me for me and didn't view me as merely a means to an end.[1]

Benefits

"Manure makes the best soil for plants to thrive." Being an MK or TCK has its challenges, but beautiful things can come out of those. Being unable to distinguish any particular country as home brings with it the very tangible feeling of being "foreigners and strangers on earth" (Hebrews 11:13). It is an opportunity not to get caught up in worldly affairs, even well-meaning but misplaced patriotism. It is an opportunity to view only heaven as home.

Adaptability

MKs also generally grow up to be quite adaptable. They have learned to accommodate multiple cultures and traditions and may be keen to distinguish between objective truth and cultural preferences. MKs often handle life changes or new circumstances well because of shifting paradigms as a child. My wife (who is not an MK) and I talk about how she has a more highly developed "sense of normalcy" than I do: when something is out of the norm, it is less likely to frustrate me than her.

Compassion

This also helps MKs sympathize with people who are not like them. Even in their passport countries, MKs find that they have noticeable cultural differences with their peers and have to learn to overcome these obstacles early. Compassion obviously requires more than just experience (it depends much more on the work of the Holy Spirit), but the MK does grow up developing a skill set that later in life may help them to better relate to foreigners, minorities, and other marginalized peoples.

Parents as godly examples

Finally, an MK grows up watching their parents follow the Lord's calling. Their natural role models get to exemplify what it looks like to radically leave behind family, friends, and comfort to follow Jesus. It may take years for the MK to understand why exactly their parents did what they did. It may take years for an MK to come to grips with what they themselves lost because of their parents' obedience. But an MK grows up not just hearing but seeing how much it's worth to follow Jesus, and a parent can ask for few things better than that for their child.

Identity

Once again, every child is different. Many MKs relate to some or all of the experiences above. Others might not relate at all. That's okay. Cultural identity is a tricky thing, and there's no formula to define it, especially in unusual situations like being an MK. Some will fully consider themselves culturally belonging to their passport country, others to their country of service, and many not quite to either. In many cases, an MK will even feel culturally different from their parents, who may more fully culturally belong to their passport country. MKs often feel most naturally connected to other MKs because of similar experiences and struggles. (This is true in my case—though at times I was even insecure in culturally being an MK because I only lived four years in my country of service.) Any of the above is acceptable. At the end of the day, MKs, like every other human being, need to find their complete identity in Christ. This doesn't annul cultural identity. Let us end with concluding that the most important thing for an MK is not to find their perfect fit in the world, but to know their perfect Savior in heaven.

Do you know an MK? Are you raising one? Don't be afraid to ask them how it has shaped/is shaping their faith and life. Chances are they will appreciate that you recognize their unique experience (actually, most people appreciate being asked about themselves). Ask if they think they've experienced the challenges above. Try to avoid generic questions like, "How was childhood in _____?" (as if they have another childhood to compare it to), and we all dread the "Which country do you like better?" question. But allow them to express themselves, even if it doesn't all add up in your mind. In the end, you may just make a friend with someone who is surprisingly different from you, in ways in which you both can learn from each other and "spur one another on toward love and good deeds" (Hebrews 10:24).

1. Note, this is a slightly different theme than righteousness by works. You can have your theology of grace all in place and still struggle to understand just how precious you are to Jesus.

About W

W spent four years as a missionary kid before his family moved back to the United States. He and his wife are currently missionaries in a creative access nation.

10

Paying the Price of Cross-Cultural Missions

Ibrahim Omondi

Cross-cultural missions is costly. But as with many things, the sacrifice is often overshadowed by the rewards—immeasurable joy and fulfillment.

What *are* the costs of being a missionary? We will identify several.

Taking a risk

Cross-cultural missions involves risk. God's heart for cross-cultural missions is depicted in these words to Abram, "Get out of your country, from your family and from your father's house, to a land that I will show you. I will make you a great nation. I will bless you, and make your name great" (Genesis 12:1–2, New King James Version [NKJV]). Abram took the risk of leaving his culture and comfort zone, but he did so joyfully, for it was in obedience to God's command. The Lord God who commanded him to go to the foreign land did not stay behind, leaving Abram alone. God was with him all along to fulfill the promises of the call.

God will not abandon the missionary of the 21st century either. But he or she must be ready to go in the footsteps of Jesus, who demands, "If anyone desires to come after me, let him deny himself, and take up his cross daily, and follow me. For whoever

51

desires to save his life will lose it. But whoever loses his life for my sake will save it" (Luke 9:23–24, NKJV).

In the church today, there are two sorts of people. One sort wishes to preserve their security and comfort, avoiding self-denial or risk-taking. The other is willing to risk everything in obedience to the Great Commission.

Standard of living

Paul says in Philippians 4:11–12 that he is content in any and every circumstance, having learned the secret of being full and being hungry. He was used to an irregular supply of funds; sometimes he had plenty, often he had little. In serving God, Paul remembers "beatings, imprisonments and riots; in hard work, sleepless nights and hunger," of being "poor, yet making many rich; having nothing, and yet possessing everything" (2 Corinthians 6:5, 10).

Jesus asks us to be willing to lose the affluence and prosperity in which we may have grown up, to be prepared to accept relative poverty and move to a simpler lifestyle. As a missionary, you do not want to appear to your new neighbors like an invader from Mars! You do not want to be a person who lives in your own space capsule with air conditioning and filtered water, eating imported food, and being isolated in a private, luxurious compound away from jostling crowds and local intrigues.

You are accustomed to having a refrigerator, washing machine, and private vehicle. Are you willing to lose even these? Are you willing to expose yourself to the sweat and heat of a semi-desert climate that is laden with flies, mosquitoes, and maybe even fleas? These may be part of your calling as a cross-cultural missionary.

Cultural privilege and status

"But what things were gain to me, these I have counted loss for Christ" (Philippians 3:7, NKJV). Paul counted all but loss. His Pharisaic upbringing, intellectual ability, Jewish pedigree—all of these meant nothing to him. This is part of the price that a missionary has to pay when moving from his or her own culture into another. Cultural assets are frozen; privileges become disadvantages.

All academic credits, cultural identity, and intellectual pride lose their value when you cross over into another culture. Your many years of church experience may mean nothing as you begin to struggle to learn and speak a new language. Your experience in this new culture is like being born again—this time as a cultural infant and linguistic idiot. At home you are somebody. You are known and appreciated. You have a place in society through your family and friends. Are you willing to become a "nobody" in a place where no one knows you? That is the risk God asks us to take.

Security and health

Paul's letter to the church in Philippi was written from a prison in what is now Eastern Europe. This was not our modern, deluxe correctional institution. It was a horrible place. Beaten, cast into the stocks, he and Silas could not run. God wanted them right where they were. It was through their suffering that the jailer was converted.

Why risk going to countries which are politically insecure, with the possibility of revolution, riots, and war? Because God wants us to be there to bless those who are going through suffering.

What about the risks Jesus took when He was born as a human baby in an unsanitary cave-stable, full of the smell of dung and urine? He could have died of infection! Yes, God chose for Him to do that and calls the missionary of the 21st century to do it as well.

Family and friends

Paul was probably disowned by his Jewish family of Tarsus when he decided to follow the Way of Jesus. Other apostles took their wives with them (1 Corinthians 9:5), but Paul did not. Timothy left his dear mother and grandmother behind in Lystra

(Philippians 2:22). Answering a call to missions meant, and still does, frequent moves from place to place. Jesus knows what human loneliness feels like. He experienced loneliness on the cross when He cried out, "My God, my God, why have you forsaken me?" Yes, He can ask us to even pay the price of separation from parents, friends, and children.

Life itself

Paul anticipated that his life would be poured out as a drink offering, as he explains in Philippians 1:20–25. Many early missionaries risked death. When missionaries went out from Europe in the 1800s and 1900s, most of them died in the first or second years of their service.

When insecurity and attacks against Christians were on the rise in areas where DOVE Africa missionaries are serving, we asked each one of them if they would want to evacuate. "We came here ready to lose our lives for Christ, and that has not changed," they declared, one after the other. Sometimes, the cost of cross-cultural missions is life itself.

Is it worth it?

When Peter says, "We have left everything to follow you," Jesus replies, "Truly I tell you, no one who has left home or brothers or sisters or mother or father or children or fields for me and the gospel will fail to receive a hundred times as much in this present age; homes, brothers, sisters, mothers, children and fields—along with persecutions—and in the age to come eternal life" (Mark 10:28–30). This is true to experience. We have to "leave" before we "receive."

Having friends, lifelong friends from different cultures, is a foretaste of heaven. As a cross-cultural missionary, you will find people in heaven who are there because you were sent to them! All "these things," here on earth, and rewards for eternity, will be added to you.

What price could the Lord be asking you to pay for the sake of His Kingdom?

About Ibrahim Omondi

Ibrahim came to the USA from Kenya in 1978 to attend college and also to study for one summer at the US Center for World Missions. He had a passion for doing missions in China. Back in Kenya, Ibrahim was involved in starting a missions training center that has trained and sent many local missionaries to least-reached people groups in Kenya. Since 2000, DOVE Africa has sent missionaries to serve among Islamic people groups. He continues to trust God and pray for an effective way to see an entire people group come to Christ in this season of mission endeavor.

11

A Bridge for the Gospel: Starting Small Businesses

Dirk Develing

It was March 2020. It was hot, really hot in northern Kenya. Even the local people said, "This is the hottest city in the country and the hottest season of the year." At that same time governments around the globe were locking down their countries because of COVID-19. For me this could mean that there would be difficulties in flying back home to the Netherlands.

Why was I in Kenya in these extreme circumstances? Together with a friend, I was in a small room with one small fan and eighteen missionaries talking and interacting about business, the gospel, missions, and church. We were training and coaching people to start a small business. And I loved it!

But how is business relevant in the conversation about cross-cultural missions? Here are three reasons.

It is biblical to have a business while being on a mission

Unlike Peter and other apostles in the early Christian church, who devoted themselves entirely to their religious ministry and lived off money donated by church members (see Acts 4:34–37), Paul often performed outside work, not desiring to be a financial burden to the young churches he founded. In Thessalonica, Paul states that he and his companions "worked night and day...so that we would not be a burden to any of you" (2 Thessalonians 3:8).

Business profit can extend the Kingdom and provide a living

Money is needed to extend the Kingdom of God. A lot of missionaries are poor. By starting a business they can not only provide food for their family, but also travel to other cities to help others and start new initiatives. All such matters become a means to extend God's Kingdom, for God is the one who provides seed for the farmer and then bread to eat (2 Corinthians 9:10).

Through business we can connect more easily with people

If we want to reach people with the gospel, we first have to get to know them. As a missionary it is far easier to have a reason to talk to them before we share the gospel. As a business owner you have to talk with people and transact business with them. It will create opportunities to make disciples. The business will be the bridge for the gospel.

In the training to missionaries we not only talk about the technical part of "running a business," but also look at the needs in the community, so we can adapt to that. We look at skills. What did God give you? We explore our view of money. Do we think money is something dirty? Or, is it neutral and can we use "God's money" for good?

We helped the people break limiting mindsets by asking questions. What if money was not an issue? What will you dream of? How big will your business be? Do you have employees? Will it only be in the region, or do you have shops all around the country?

It is so exciting to hear the big dreams, like "starting a sesame seed oil plant" or "a mobile dryer" to solve the problem of rotten mangoes. Before how-tos are worked out, we begin with bigger dreams and seeing the possibilities.

Church and business are very close to each other

Because of culture and tradition we can see church as the sphere of spiritual activity, while business is something completely separate. A closer look, however, reveals the spiritual nature of business. We can worship while working in our business. We can have fellowship with our customers, our employees, our business partners. We can make disciples in a way that is not "project oriented." We can give money out of our business to bless people and God. We can share and show biblical qualities to others as we engage in business. Thus, in many situations we can do the ministry of the church while running a business.

Let's renew our minds and discover this bridge that God gave to extend His Kingdom!

About Dirk Develing

Dirk is from the Netherlands. He is bi-vocational, both running an online marketing consultancy business and also leading a church. He serves on the DOVE Europe leadership team and often travels to other nations helping Christians with disciple-making, church planting, and developing businesses.

12

Open Heart, Open Home

Nancy Leatherman

As a child being raised in south central Pennsylvania, I was intrigued by stories of missionaries living in a culture much different from my own. While a high school student, I wondered which Spanish-speaking country I might live in when I grew up. After completing an education degree, I moved to Jamaica to teach at a deaf school. Although it was a challenge to learn sign language after I arrived in Kingston, my two flatmates gave encouragement and the camaraderie I needed.

My next cultural challenge was teaching school in inner-city Philadelphia. What a wonderful world for me—new people to live with, new norms to accept, and ways of life to explore.

While there, I met a young man volunteering in the city; he later became my husband. One attraction was that he previously had a college semester abroad in Belize and was interested in church work and possibly international missions, too. Before our first wedding anniversary, we settled into an apartment in Belize City with an assignment to work with youth group leaders. The next four years we assisted various churches and lived in three different districts, each culturally different using unique spoken languages (English Creole, Spanish, and Garifuna, even though the national language is English).

Forced to return to my home country

Suddenly, life changed when my husband, Duane, returned from a weekend outreach in the seaside town of Seine Bight. He was very weak and unable to walk. Quickly we returned to the United States to receive medical care in Miami Beach, Florida. May 3rd I tried to celebrate his 26th birthday in that intensive care room, not knowing that he would be comatose several days later due to a medical accident. Duane, Brian (our 19-month-old son) and I (eight months pregnant with our second child) were transported via air ambulance to Lancaster, Pennsylvania, later that month. I welcomed our newborn, Beth, into our family three weeks later.

Our overseas mission assignment abruptly ended. My husband lived in a coma at the local hospital for the following 15 ½ years while I raised our two children. As you can imagine, my mission work changed significantly. I returned to Dangriga in Belize nine months later simply to pack up a few suitcases and leave our mission house to another couple.

Blessing the nations from home

Can I be a missionary if I need to stay stateside, take care of babies, and make visits to the hospital to hopefully comfort or encourage a comatose young father? Yes! I believe it's possible. It was my life.

I was certainly not residing where I expected and not co-ministering with my husband in small villages, training young national church leaders, nor singing worship songs in Garifuna or Spanish. However, through those years, many ICU staff knew I faithfully read the Scriptures, played Christian music, and would pray with Duane daily in that hospital room. Sometimes staff and family members of those in nearby rooms asked about my faith.

During these years when I couldn't live overseas, I hosted Japanese students in my home, taught small ESL classes, and tutored international students who came to Lancaster County to learn about the American way of life and be exposed to Christianity. You could say the mission field came to me. The gift of hospitality was expressed as I opened my doors to international visitors and served dinners around my kitchen or dining room tables. Whether it was helping a teen practice English conversation or increase their cultural understanding, I shared God's love and Scriptures with the students as they interacted with my family and others.

Where is your field of mission outreach? Consider making your house a mission place. Shine the love of God right where you are. Let the world know Jesus is real to you, even from your home.

About Nancy Leatherman

Nancy served other cultures by teaching at a deaf school in Kingston, Jamaica, and an inner-city school in Philadelphia, PA. She and her late husband served in Belize training young church leaders. After returning to the USA she worked with international students through American Home Life International and as an administrative assistant at Eastern Mennonite Missions, Teaching The Word Ministries, and DOVE Mission International. She is mother of two adult children and grandmother of two.

13

Medical Missions: From Dispensing Expertise to Collaborative Partnership

Dr. T. Scott Jackson, M.D.

As with most practices and perspectives, with time and experience coupled with changes in cultural norms and ideas, things change. I had a college spiritual mentor tell me many times, "change or die." I do not totally agree that life is that simple, but there is much truth in the directive. Some say that we need to "swim with the current or get out of the water." No matter how one states the thought, we would all do well to take a good inventory of what is cutting edge in whatever journey we are on. We must always couple this with the direction in which God is leading us before coming up with our own final perspective.

When it comes to medical missions, the same thoughts apply. I can remember some twenty years ago traveling to Haiti with grandiose ideas of participating in medical missions. I would dream of being the next Albert Schweitzer who was a famous German theologian, musician, writer, humanitarian, philosopher, and physician. I first was introduced to the legend at the famous Albert Schweitzer Hospital in Des Chapelle, Haiti, which was started by D. Richard Mellon and was named after Dr. Schweitzer. For years I would organize teams, sometimes several per year, with the "medical model" of one or more physicians, several nurses, at least one pharmacist, and multiple helpers who could man the pharmacy as well as handle prayer needs for the local patients that were being served.

This model worked successfully for many years both in Haiti and other locales such as Guatemala, Kenya, Uganda, Ghana, and Kurdish Iraq. At times, attempts were made to teach basic health principles and best practice techniques to the local citizens. There were even some successful efforts to sponsor some young Haitian adults to complete schooling in a health care program in their local city. By far and wide, however, we fostered dependence on the American tradition of planting a team for a short-term event caring for as many patients as possible in an allotted time. (I know there are American and international institutions who have been planted long-term in a region to invest time, money, and manpower to raise up qualified native health care workers to take over the helm. I am mainly speaking from my own experience in "doing" medical missions for the past twenty years.)

As time progressed, our teams often lacked the full complement of the "perfect" type of health care worker, causing us to stretch each participant's job description such that it was not uncommon to have a nurse perform his or her usual duties and include that of a pharmacist, prayer partner, crowd controller, or even physician at times. I am not convinced that we did a poor job in recruitment of necessary mission participants, but this would become a natural flow of how missions in general is evolving. I would like to think that God being the author and finisher of our faith has directed such changes for the betterment of all concerned.

It seems that in the realm of medical missions, we all must be open to change. Several observations have seemed to occur no matter what region of the world we serve. The biggest change is that of "partnering with the local community." In that statement, I am referring to recruiting local team members to work alongside our team. That would include physicians, nurses, lab technicians, pastors, teachers, interpreters, and general helpers. It seems that there is a "buy-in" factor that helps to guarantee a successful mission endeavor. With that local involvement, one often sees better results, as there is more general cultural acceptance, better follow-up, and overall better compliance.

Partnering with the local community also involves utilizing the local resources in terms of pharmaceuticals, supplies, even local meeting establishments including schools, churches, and clinics. Communication has evolved to the point that we can easily plan from most any location in the US to any place in the world that has access to texting or online platforms.

I believe that a much more balanced approach to medical missions is happening throughout the world today. It is indeed taking the emphasis off the traditional missionary style of medicine and forming a new cooperative style. This style is recognizing the talents and abilities of the local populations and coming alongside people to help teach and encourage them to serve their own needs. I believe this type of perspective is God directed and will foster greater long-term improvement in our health care quest for the world around us. Each of us must be open to change as we seek to carry out the directive of spreading the gospel of Jesus Christ to everyone's world.

About Dr. T. Scott Jackson, M.D.

Dr. Scott Jackson has served as a family practice physician since 1985 and has experienced the compassion of God moving through international medical missions for many of those years. He helped found DOVE Medical Missions and has led medical teams throughout the world including Haiti, Guatemala, Peru, Kenya, Uganda, and Iraq.

14

Meeting Jesus through a Social Media Ad
Using Today's Technologies

R & M

"How, then, can they call on the one they have not
believed in? And how can they believe in the one
of whom they have not heard? And how can they hear
without someone preaching to them?"

Romans 10:14

Imagine this scenario: Adam[1] was curious. He'd grown up believing in Allah, but as he got older he found himself questioning Islam. Eventually he came to a point where he no longer considered himself a Muslim. And yet, he still wondered if there was a God. Was there something he was missing? So he began searching. He didn't know any Christians. Furthermore, in the country he lived in it wasn't legal for him to leave Islam, much less go to a church. All of the churches for local believers were underground.

One day as he was scrolling through his newsfeed on Facebook, he came across an advertisement asking, "Is what you believe true, and does it bring you peace? Learn more about Jesus the Messiah who said, 'I am the way the truth and the life' and promises peace for all who believe in Him!"

A carefully designed automated messaging service offers

Adam information, videos, verses, and questions with the option to continue learning, or talk to a real person. Adam eagerly clicks through, excited and absorbing what he is seeing and reading. Eventually he is asked if he'd like to meet with a believer in person to talk more.

This story is true, not only in one location. This is happening around the globe. Every day people like Adam click through these advertisements and are connected with a believer and begin studying God's Word. In the case of Adam, he is now doing a Discovery Bible Study with another believer and learning what it would mean for him to follow Jesus. He is so excited about what he is learning; he has even brought along a friend to learn with him.

Technology goes where we often cannot

The nation where Adam lives has over 32 million people and only .001% are believers. Would Adam have been able to connect with a believer were it not for this interactive ad? We understand that of course it is *possible* (for with God all things are possible), but God is using social media as an avenue for people to hear truth.

We live in an amazing day and age where we can connect with anyone anytime, and in any part of the world. This has often been lamented; many are swearing off social media all together. We don't need to go into all of the shortcomings of social media, but for all of the challenges and pitfalls, God is using it to proclaim who He is.

There are so many places in the world where it is actually illegal to proclaim the good news. In these places there are few believers, and most are forced to meet in underground churches, needing to be careful how they share their faith with others. Because these places are hard for foreign missionaries to access, there are few missionaries there. The ratio of nonbelievers to believers is extremely high. What are the chances of a seeker coming into contact with a believer? Not very high. So how do you find those who are seeking? How do you find those who are hungry and searching?

For years, radio and television have been used as one way to reach people in creative access nations. Now, an ever-increasing number of people are actively online. Places like YouTube, Instagram, and Facebook are highly popular. We've spent the last several years living in a country where it is illegal to proselytize and where the percentage of Christians is below 1%. We are continually trying to create opportunities to share and gauge spiritual interest as we meet people at grocery stores, gyms, in taxis, and so on. This is important, and something we will continue doing. Along the way we have made different friends and connections. However, with a media tool that uses online ads and social media, we're able to engage with hundreds in one weekend! All across our country and in other creative access nations, people who love Jesus and follow him are turning to media as a way to share the gospel and find those who are seeking truth.

In each case the ultimate goal is to get to a face-to-face meeting so that the interested person can meet with a believer and study the Word together. Ideally, as in our context, this is done in relationship with a locally led church. When the individual is ready and the church leader is confident that this new believer's faith is genuine, they are able to join a local church and continue their discipleship journey.

Next time you're scrolling through social media, take a moment and pray for these media projects. Pray that those who are seeking truth would click on these ads and pursue knowing more about Jesus. Before you bemoan the woes of this social media age, pause and ask that God would use all of these things for His glory. And maybe look into your own social media account and evaluate how you are using it to point to Christ.

1. Not his real name.

About R & M

R & M are workers in a creative access nation.

15

Chopsticks vs. Forks

Wes Dudley

One of the obvious realities of visiting another country is that you are presented with a totally different way of doing things. Whether you want to admit it or not, your national, local, and family culture has influenced just about everything you do—and likely *why* you do it in the first place. From the simplest of family traditions such as singing Christmas carols around the tree, to the independent nature of most Americans, or even the way we interpret the Bible, we're all connected to different sets of values, practices, and habits that have shaped the way we think. That's why spending time in other nations or with others from various countries is one of the best ways to discover that there are many beautiful and fulfilling cultures—cultures quite different from your own.

An American in Taiwan

I had the privilege of living in Taiwan for about four years, and it was without a doubt the most eye-opening experience of my life. For me, it illuminated some of the unhealthy preconceived notions and ideas that were shaped by my own culture, and it helped provide me with a completely different perspective when working alongside those who think differently than me. Hopefully you can relate to this if you have ever traveled outside your home country. The new smells, sights, languages, and local traditions have the potential to amaze you and help you discover that there are completely different ways of effectively living life.

God and dinner

For example, if you have spent any time in countries located in Eastern Asia, such as Taiwan, then you will notice quite quickly that their way of enjoying a meal together is much different than those residing in the West. In America, whenever you eat out, the food primarily is prepared for your plate alone. There is meaning to this. A plate is set before me, and the food that is flirting with me is for my mouth only—merely exemplifying the individualistic tendencies of our Western culture. However, in Taiwan, most often all of the food is placed in the middle of the table, and then friends "dive in" together with their chopsticks to share bites of tasty morsels all while ensuing in hearty dialog. Many times, there is even a large rotating tray in the middle of the table, allowing everyone to share food dishes easily. It was always fun to see Americans experience this Taiwanese style for the first time as everyone's chopsticks went to work and the turntable started spinning furiously.

Does it really matter how you eat your food, though? Well, while I'm not going to say that one culture trumps the other, I do appreciate the Taiwanese perspective for one primary reason: it focuses on the relationship! Instead of encouraging you to look down at your own plate while you seek to scarf your food down, the Taiwanese approach reminds you that the mealtime is more about the friendships than just the food—because isn't that what it's really all about anyway? Even in the Middle East, we see Jesus' example of breaking bread and passing it along to His disciples. It's easy to come to love the Taiwanese way of dining together, even though it stands in stark contrast to the way that many Westerners grow up. You will find that this collective approach gives everyone a chance to taste some of the same things, and creates even more opportunities to have quality fellowship.

Many of us can connect to God in the same way that we approach our dinner plate. Our God created us for relationship and He longs for us to know Him, but we don't always desire Him for who He is because we see Him as a useful instrument for acquiring something better. So often, instead of pursuing our "friend," we focus only on the "food," and thereby miss out on what the "meal" is all about. Skye Jethani puts it beautifully in his book *With* when he says that if our vision were enlarged and corrected, God "would cease to be *how we acquire* our treasure, and he would *become* our treasure" (emphasis in original). Are we enjoying life with Him simply because of who He is, or is it more about the delicious taste of life that we are hoping to get from Him?

Regardless if you prefer forks over chopsticks, we are all part of a wonderfully diverse and creative world that God has uniquely designed, and we can do ourselves a huge disservice by not taking the time to notice the different ways to think or simply live life. No one specific culture trumps another, and participating in short-term mission trips, reading books that illuminate cultural perspectives, or just building relationships with those from other nations are great ways to expand our perspective—and even help us evaluate the way that we approach God.

About Wes Dudley

Wes has served as the missions director at DOVE Westgate Church since 2013 and has had the opportunity to participate with many short-term mission teams, as well as prepare and commission numerous long-term missionaries. He and his wife, Julianna, lived in Taiwan for over four years as missionary teachers of English as a second language. Wes has a passion for networking with believers from other nations. He currently resides in Ephrata, Pennsylvania.

16

Children as Missionaries

Josie Wilson

Does God call children to the mission field? Can God use children in missions? Absolutely!

The Great Commission does not mention age

Missions is God's heart for us all, no matter our age. The Great Commission in Matthew 28:19–20, does not specify an age. We are all capable of going where God tells us to go and do what He tells us to do, children included.

There are many facets of missions, both in our homeland and abroad. Some are called to leave their homeland, while others are called to stay, pray, and support those who are called to go. Just because God hasn't called us to go, doesn't mean the Great Commission does not apply. We can do plenty to reflect God's missionary heart right where we are, such as serving others, feeding the hungry, clothing the poor, and sharing Jesus in practical ways to those around us. Such things, along with giving our finances, are all ways we can be used by God to build His Kingdom. Are we doing these things as a husband and wife? As a family unit? Don't allow your kids to miss out.

Our kids have the very same Jesus within them. Their spirit is no smaller. They are capable of hearing and experiencing God as we are. Are we allowing our children to participate in missions? When God is in it, there is nothing too small or insignificant. It takes mustard seed faith, the smallest of seeds. Our children are not too young or too small. Don't wait for them to reach their late teen years so they can go on a mission team with the youth group. Help them cultivate God's heart for missions as a young child. They can be involved by supporting a missionary, or praying for those in other nations.

Going to a foreign land is not always the direction God leads us into, but if He does, are you willing to allow your kids to experience what God has for them? Moreover, allow God to use your children to touch other lives for Him. When we go in obedience, God blesses our going. We may not see much fruit with our eyes, but remember, we are planting seeds in obedience to the calling.

I spent much of my later teens into my 20s focused on missions. I would take a trip, then return home to work and raise money to go on another trip. After many short-term mission trips, I was led into two long-term commitments. On that last mission commitment, I met my husband, who is originally from Ohio. I left my heart for missions on the back burner as we remained in the USA and our focus became family. Together we are raising our three children to have a heart for missions, as we both have gone on multiple trips to foreign lands. Our heart for missions never died, but continued to grow as we supported missionaries and prayed for the proper timing and finances to go, not individually, but as a family. To date, our children, ages 13 and below, have been to East Africa twice.

Kids on cross-cultural mission

During the summer of 2019, our family, together with another family, served in Kenya and Uganda. I was encouraged to see how God used the children, ages ranging from 9 to 17. For example, they helped to paint a village school in Kenya and a church building in Kampala, Uganda. The team also ministered to schoolchildren by sharing Bible stories and teaching and playing soccer. The children were even able to minister to the team driver. He jumped right in helping to paint, working on service projects and playing soccer with the kids. He didn't mind getting dirty. Although he had been raised in a Christian family, he walked away from his upbringing as a teenager. After spending a few days as an additional member of our mission team, his love for the Lord was renewed and he invited Jesus back into his life. We praise God that we all were able to be part of what God was doing in the life of this man. Aaron, 11, connected with the local children through playing soccer. Naomi, 13, enjoyed visiting a school in Nairobi and interacting with the girls, playing games, and learning about them. She learned that many children grow up multi-lingual as she interacted with young children learning their third language! Allison, 11, reported: "I enjoyed doing Bible lessons with the kids in a village in Kenya and at church in Uganda." The lives of all of the children were impacted: Kenyan, Ugandan, and American.

My husband, Mark, as a child, also participated in multiple family mission teams. Through such participation, he learned to speak in public at a young age, to appreciate other cultures, to love people different from him, and to reach out to others with the love of Jesus in countries where things were not always as safe as back home. These trips helped shape him into the man of God he is today.

Allowing God to use our children

Many years ago, God used me to change my mother's heart concerning missions. As a teenager, my mom feared the call to go to Africa. God worked through that fear, giving me a heart for Africa and sent me. My mom was then able to face that fear and experience Africa herself because of my going. God wants to use our children! I personally do not want to stand in the way. Will you give Him full permission?

About Josie Wilson

Josie's missions experience started as a teenager when she served on a team in Scotland. After graduating from high school, she led several short-term teams to various nations in Africa, and served long-term in Kenya and Uganda. Josie and her husband, Mark, along with their three children, reside in Womelsdorf, PA. Josie serves as missions representative at her church and serves on the DMI leadership team. Josie continues to lead missions teams to East Africa.

17

Can Evangelism and Social Justice Get Along?

Justin Shrum

In July 1974, over 2,500 Christian leaders came together from over 150 countries for the First International Congress on World Evangelization at Lausanne, Switzerland. Among many other outcomes, this historic event produced The Lausanne Covenant.[1]

The Lausanne Covenant is a type of modern creed which has offered many evangelical churches and movements a shared statement of belief. Since it was a uniquely missional creed, the goal was to build missions and evangelism into the heart of the Christian confession. As such, six of the fifteen points provide statements to the various dynamics related to evangelism.

It might thus be perplexing for some that embedded within the statements given to defining and articulating various points on evangelism, the covenant has a section specifically titled "Christian Social Responsibility." The third sentence brings the two elements together, saying, "Here too we express penitence both for our neglect and for having sometimes regarded evangelism and social concern as mutually exclusive."

John Stott, a British theologian, gives additional insight, saying that a large number of the participants wanted to communicate the above point more strongly, to emphasis the lifestyle-shaping role of discipleship. They had proposed, "We must repudiate as demonic the attempt to drive a wedge between evangelism and social action."[2] Ultimately, the assembly chose a milder but broader expression. Nevertheless, they also accurately identified a challenge within modern Christianity which has remained to this day.

To what challenge were they explicitly referring? The tendency that the Church has had to move between the conceptualizations of evangelism and social action as mutually exclusive elements of the gospel.

Mutual suspicion

Have you noticed this tendency? It doesn't take long to recognize it within our current public discourse, especially on social media. It is common now to see posts coming from each side, where views are offered not just to challenge the other side but to silence them. The evangelism side often accuses social action of disregarding the spiritual for the material, of being too influenced by societal trends and replacing the gospel with political ideology. The social action side, in turn, accuses the emphasis on evangelism of ignoring concrete human needs, of reducing the gospel to soul-escapism, and of disregarding the sociopolitical dynamics related to our church communities. Above all, both sides are suspicious that the other is simply using the gospel as a cover for their own agenda.

Global theological voices

When the authors wrote their text in 1974, the Church in the Global North had already been experiencing this two-sided debate. At that time, many were in a season of reaction against the "social gospel" which had been the trend at the turn of the 20th century. The two world wars had brought a new consciousness of the need for evangelism and disillusionment with the apparent failure of an emphasis on the social good of the gospel. The baby boomer generation, born into this widespread disillusionment as well as the miraculous establishment of the modern state of Israel, experienced an unparalleled urgency for evangelism and mission.

At nearly the same time, new theological views were beginning to arise in South America. In response to disappointment with how relief and aid from the Global North were being used to support corrupt regimes, a Peruvian priest and theologian named Gustavo Gutiérrez introduced a theological approach called "liberation theology." In this approach, "the poor" are not only the subject of God's concern (expressed in Christian charity) but are presented as God's people based on their historical victimization (invoking the idea of solidarity). Based on God's commitment to the poor, the Church is expected to stand on behalf of their social and political needs. As liberation theology spread into new contexts over the last 40 years, new groups—such as black liberation theology and feminist theology—found meaning in the idea of God working with them to better their real social and political disadvantages.

Unfortunately, the trajectories of these two views have only deepened further the "demonic" divide between evangelism and social action. There appear to be fewer communities willing to traverse the middle ground. Like the tragic picture of children torn between two hardened, divorced parents and now assigned the miserable role of communicating between the two, the mutual exclusion of these two dynamics of the gospel is toxic. It remains a threat to the growth and maturity of the Body of Christ.

The stance of the Lausanne Covenant

The Lausanne Covenant pursued having both evangelism and social action stand shoulder to shoulder in a mature dialogue with one another. They presented these two elements of the gospel with the concept of "dialectics." This concept relies heavily on the metaphor of two opposing individuals having a productive discussion with one another. The implications are that ideas and principles are best developed through robust and reasoned dialogue. Indeed, this reflects an entirely different spirit to the currently trending "cancel culture," where ideas and arguments are used as weapons to silence the views of others instead of engaging them. Unfortunately, cancel culture is not unique to one side of our raging political debate, nor is it absent from the Church.

For the apostle Paul, it is precisely the capacity the saints have to speak to one another which determines the unity and the maturity of the Church:

"Until we all attain to the unity of the faith and of the knowledge of the Son of God, to mature manhood, . . . *so that we may no longer be children,* tossed to and fro by the waves and carried about by every wind of doctrine, by human cunning, by craftiness in deceitful schemes. Rather, *speaking the truth in love, we are to grow up*" (Ephesians 4:13–15, ESV, emphasis added).

When applying this image to social action and evangelism, we ought to expect that a mature body, as it encounters various strongholds, can carry both social engagement and evangelism as elements of the gospel. Instead of being shaped by the world's division between the two, whether political or hyper-spiritual, the mature body remains in dialogue with itself.

The Kingdom of God

This question remains to be asked: how can we legitimately argue that evangelism and social action belong in the same room as valuable conversation partners? It would undoubtedly take a thick book to make a case for both of these elements and to examine the biblical history of their inter-relationship. Since such a thing is far beyond what I have committed to write and what you are committed to read, I will simply use one fundamental claim: the proclamation and ministry of Jesus. "Now after John was arrested, Jesus came into Galilee, proclaiming the gospel of God, and saying, 'The time is fulfilled, and the Kingdom of God is at hand; repent and believe in the gospel'" (Mark 1:14–15, ESV).

After returning from exile, the Jewish community in Israel became enamored of the hope of God's intervention through the person of the Messiah. As this hope became more concrete, Jewish holiness began to center around the idea of legitimacy for the inheritance of the coming Kingdom. The idea goes like this: the Messiah is going to come and bring about the resurrection of the dead, the end of the age and will also grant the Kingdom as an inheritance to the faithful. So only those faithful in the exact right way will be counted worthy. Much of Jewish sectarianism of Jesus' day appears to be centered on in-fighting related to the question of who is worthy to attain the inheritance of the Kingdom.

The above passage in Mark presents how Jesus dynamically introduced the gospel in the form of an invitation to inherit God's soon-coming Kingdom. The idiomatic phrase "at hand" was used to describe something which was just about to happen. We use the phrase "just around the corner." We can see how Jesus' proclamation thus includes an "already but not yet" element. In other words, the declaration of the gospel through Jesus was an invitation to become those who will soon inherit God's Kingdom. The miracle of God's grace is that Jesus places being worthy for the inheritance of the Kingdom to the simple act of turning to Him in trusting loyalty ("repent and believe").

Empowerment and inclusion

What is more, the redefined concept of attaining the inheritance empowered the poor, a group of people who had found themselves as social outsiders due to their defects (Luke 4:16–21). The same goes for those who found jobs as tax collectors or were in prostitution because of the threat of poverty. Those whose social circumstances meant being shut out were now being brought in through Jesus' gracious proclamation. He not only invited people into a personal experience of becoming an heir in the Kingdom, but He also created a new social collective around that coming reality. Furthermore, He created a shared purse within this community to begin caring for the practical needs of those who had embraced His proclamation with believing loyalty.

This brief look at the intersection of evangelism and social action in the ministry and proclamation of Jesus reminds us that these elements are indeed two sides of one gospel coin. The Church must continue what Jesus began: to engage the world in the power of the Spirit, anticipating the Spirit to move by both bringing new heirs into the Kingdom and by empowering new social realities!

1. If you haven't read it yet, please take the time to read and reflect on this valuable expression of Christian unity around the call to mission and evangelism. https://www.lausanne.org/content/covenant/lausanne-covenant

2. John Stott. *The Lausanne Covenant: An Exposition and Commentary.* (Lausanne Occasional Paper 3). (1975). Available at: https://www.lausanne.org/content/lop/lop-3.

About Justin Shrum

Justin and his wife, Rawan, lead an anti-human trafficking organization in Karlsruhe, Germany, named The Justice Project. This organization assists West African victims of human trafficking and also Eastern European women working in Germany's legalized sex industry. Since the Shrums received a clear calling from God to serve long-term in a field of social work, they have often wrestled with the gospel's relevance for social issues.

18

Youth Missions:
Coming Back Changed

Stephanie Sauder

Some may wonder whether more happens in the lives of those participating in a short-term missions team than in the lives of those the team aims to serve. Rather than compare these two aspects, or see them as mutually exclusive, perhaps there is no dichotomy—both are true! Both can be signs of God's transformation through the mission team. When I began to participate in missions as teenager, I learned that as I sought to serve others, I received so much in return as God changed me.

A thirteen-year-old on a mission!

My first short-term missions trip was to Ohio. I was thirteen years old—I was there to make a difference! I had come from afar, the whole way from Pennsylvania! I had a message of hope and love. I was ready to conquer the world for God. As our team served together, I loved the way we began to operate like a family. This was when my world began to grow beyond the map of vacations I had been on with my parents. When you travel on a short-term team, you connect with the areas you visit in a way that vacationers miss out on. Reading about and then seeing a culture is great, but experiencing it with someone to whom it belongs not only teaches but changes you as well, giving you a better understanding of the world.

Whatever the reasons that someone joins a mission team, the experience puts an individual in a new, uncomfortable environment without the endless distractions of daily life. Being in a foreign environment puts us in a unique position to encounter God, humbling us and revealing truth about our lives and our relationship with the Father. Experiencing a culture for the first time tears down our defenses, leaving our hearts open to what the Father has for us. I have found this to be true on multiple occasions. While serving, God is continually working in your heart. Sometimes it takes focusing on others for us to understand what the Lord has for us. Our distractions are so loud that when we remove them, it can be surprising what we can suddenly hear.

I have found that it is hard to ignore what God is speaking to me when I am on unfamiliar soil. A year after the Ohio trip, I joined a youth team to Peru where, despite not knowing Spanish, the Lord broke down walls inside me that I did not even know that I had built. We were incredibly busy the entire time, so when we had quiet time for devotions, I was able to engage immediately in what I was reading. The whole week I worked hard and was continually pushed outside of my comfort zone as we did work projects and outreach. On our last day, I could feel something shift inside of me. I understood just a fraction of the love the Father has for the people of Peru and for me, and my heart broke. I remember that moment as clear as if it happened yesterday. It taught me to be more sensitive to the Holy Spirit and to the environment around me.

Lessons learned

Each time I have participated on a missions team, I learned some hard lessons which have shaped my life. Some are practical lessons about traveling. For example, even if you are going somewhere hot and humid, take a sweatshirt along or you may end up staying the night in the coldest part of the airport in shorts and a T-shirt! It can be pretty hard to sleep in air conditioning after a week in the Caribbean when you are trying to use your towel as a blanket.

From individual to team

Short-term teams are just that: teams. Becoming a part of a team and traveling with them creates lasting bonds despite only being together for a temporary mission. These teams have taught me about working together as a group. I have never liked wearing matching or team T-shirts, but the fifteen-year-old me absolutely despised it! So, I was appalled when our leaders decided we would be wearing our bright green team shirts to travel to Bulgaria, a trip which would take us about 24 hours including a layover. So, I stubbornly wore a sweatshirt over the shirt the entire way. Yes, it was summer, and yes, I was hot! I did not want to be seen as a part of the group; wearing my sweatshirt was a silent rebellion towards the team. But during this trip, I learned how to put aside my preferences for the sake of the team and joyfully contribute to the team effort.

The importance of prayer

The first team I led was one of the most personally challenging things I have ever done. As a result I grew spiritually, more than I ever had before. One specific lesson was about preparation; I learned just how important it is to pray and prepare. On that short-term team, I could feel each prayer we had said in preparation empower and support us. The difference prayer made was tangible and unforgettable.

The value of short-term mission teams

So, what is the value of a short-term missions team? The value is the countless lives that can be transformed, whether it be the people who support and pray for team members, those who host and support the team on the ground, or the people whom the team meets in the airport or the bus station. The value of a short-term missions trip is in the people touched by what the team is doing in their community. It is in the testimonies the team shares when they go home, and it is God's transformation in the lives of those who participate in the mission team.

About Stephanie Sauder

Stephanie has been a part of many missions teams, including teams to parts of Europe, South America, the Caribbean, and Africa. She has a desire to see lasting international relationships built and has a heart for godly community.

19

The Unexpected Rewards of Lovingly Serving Others

Lynn Ironside

The decision to join a short-term missions team may evoke numerous, often roller coaster responses as you prepare to go off to a distant neighborhood or a faraway nation, praying and desiring to embark on an adventure that will impact lives for Christ and bring about great change. The physical elements of the mission will provide a sense of great accomplishment. Building a playground for needy children or repairing a widow's mud hut so her home is no longer exposed to the heavy African rains (when they eventually come) is highly satisfying. These ostensibly tangible outcomes may appear to be the highlight of such a journey, yet I have come to understand that the spiritual elements of a missions trip will leave a much greater impact, whether we recognize it or not.

Last year, I found myself sitting at a table during a Christian conference with a group of women I did not know—all of us in our mid-forties through sixties. We were seeking to find common ground and chatted about our various interests. Each of us expressed a desire to bring Christ's love to those around us, wanting to be wherever God might place us. A dear Haitian pastor friend of mine joined us and I asked him what he might see this grouping of women being able to offer to his community. Without hesitation, he replied that he would be overjoyed to have us come to the school he oversees in Haiti to spend time with the children, encouraging them, listening to their stories, and speaking into their lives. He also envisioned us meeting the parents and praying over them. He saw what we have to offer—maturity, wisdom, gentle encouragement, loving kindness. There was no mention of us building new desks or painting the walls or sewing new uniforms for the children. My friend knew quite well that we could do any of these activities if necessary and often such actions are exactly what is needed and best addressed by a short-term missions team. He, however, saw an opportunity to invest spiritually in the lives of the children and their families and he deemed this of greater value.

Looking back on my own missions experiences, I now see how the Lord gently eased me into developing confidence in trusting His purposes. I am reminded of the words in Isaiah 64:8. "But now, O Lord, you are our Father, we are the clay, and you are our potter; we are all the work of your hand" (ESV).

Stretched beyond my usual capabilities

On earlier mission trips, I often found myself immersed in activities that were completely outside of my skill set and usually involving demanding physical labor. One summer I joined a team heading to Mediaș, Romania, to renovate an old building that was being transformed into a community center. Alongside our Romanian hosts, our Canadian team would arrive at the site in the early morning and work through until the supper hour. Most nights we would collapse in bed before ten, thankful for the rest. My initial assignment involved climbing a steep ladder and clamoring about in the loft to add bats of insulation under the slate tile roof. It was summer and the temperature in my enclosed workspace would quickly become uncomfortably hot. I soon learned how to gently push up on the slate to create a small breezy port hole as I balanced on the rafters, unrolling the insulation, and carefully setting it into place. Each morning, I would start out wearing rubber gloves but within a short time they would be slick with sweat and they would invariably slide off my fingers. Upon completion of this singular duty, I moved on to assisting others to lay a tile floor in the same building. My responsibility: carting endless buckets of cold water back and forth for the tradesmen, who initially did not trust me to do much else other than this arduous, but necessary task. During this two-week mission, I also learned how to splash watered-down whitewash on old wooden fences during the hottest temperatures on record. I regretted not having brought a few cans of good quality paint in my suitcase. I helped to install drywall and had a small part in designing a bathroom that would accommodate a wheelchair. As the days passed, it was a delight to see the building being transformed under our hands. 1 Peter 4:10 states, "Every believer has received grace gifts, so use them to serve one another as faithful stewards of the many colored tapestry of God's grace" (The Passion Translation [TPT]).

Even though I had no identifiable renovation experience, I was eager and willing to assist with whatever it was that needed doing. My confidence, however, was challenged by our site foreman, a stern man in his mid-forties who did not speak English. He would often watch me at my task and more than once, with a definite look of frustration, he would approach and attempt to redirect the way I was holding a drill or hammering a nail. I suspect he likely thought he could have finished the task in half the time.

Trusting God to guide me through unknown territory, I prayed that He would provide me the physical strength to complete the tasks at hand. If, prior to traveling I had been asked to share my résumé to support the team's planned activities, I might not have been included, yet there I was. There is such truth in the phrase, "We are called to be the hands and feet of Jesus."

Building international bonds through prayer and collaboration

Missions is all about trusting God. Participating on a mission trip is all about learning to deny oneself. If you are willing, you will discover how to respond from a place of trusting God and not your own humanness. Let me explain. Each morning, before we started working, the entire team would gather around a large table to discuss the activities of the day and pray. Most of us could not understand the prayers of the Romanian workers, nor they ours, but there was beauty in sharing this special occasion each day.

One morning, after we had been together over a week, our Romanian host asked if we would be receptive to share some of what we were sensing from the Lord. He also kindly offered to interpret our words. What transpired next has left a permanent mark on my heart. Our site supervisor started to speak and initially I assumed he was likely going to express his frustration at the many delays caused by our presence. Instead what he shared was his own life story. His background involved abuse and alcohol and much distrust. His face was somber as he spoke of the darkness of his earlier life and then he began to describe how Jesus had turned his life completely around. Even if I had not been able to understand his words, his change in countenance and the tears on his face would have been enough to convince me that this man loved Jesus with all his heart.

At one point he motioned to me and I thought, "Oh here we go! He is going to say something about my work skill now—perhaps how God has taught him to be patient because of my ineptitude." Instead, he spoke of his puzzlement that this middle-aged woman would be willing to come to Romania with obviously younger folk on a work team. Through the interpreter, he spoke of how he could see Christ within me, in my willingness to serve with joy, regardless of the task. Describing his own desires to serve Jesus, he then asked if we would pray for him. It was but a moment and yet, during that time of prayer, with words I can no longer recall, I knew this was why I had come to Romania.

Everyone contributes

Yes, I was participating on a team that came prepared to spend long days on a construction site, but this was not our only purpose. During the off hours, we visited rural villages and found numerous opportunities to bless and serve through worship and fellowship. Each moment spent offering prayer was as valuable as the completed structure we left behind, and each of us had something to contribute.

I have a quote tucked into my Bible written by Kelly Minter from a study on Nehemiah. It reads, "Anytime God reaches into time, space or history to accomplish something for us, we find ourselves in the midst of a miracle."[1] I would add that He accomplishes the miraculous *through us* if we will acknowledge our fears and limitations and trust the Holy Spirit to use us anyway.

May you never find yourself doubting your place or your worth on a mission team. Pause and remember to define your presence and your purpose as God would have you do.

"What you hold, may you always hold.
What you do, may you always do and never abandon,
but with swift pace and light step and feet unstumbling,
So that even your steps stir up no dust,
Go forward securely, joyfully and swiftly
On the path of prudent happiness."
–Clare of Assisi

1. Kelly Minter. *Nehemiah: A Heart that Can Break.* (2012), p.81.

About Lynn Ironside

Lynn's experience in missions has brought her to many new communities within Canada and internationally. She has served on teams in Canada, Bulgaria, Romania, the Netherlands, Kenya, India, Great Britain, and Colombia. She has a heart desire to pray for and minister to women of all ages, sharing of God's love for them and encouraging their sense of creativity and worth. Lynn resides in Ontario, Canada.

20

Teachers as Students: Education in a Cross-Cultural Setting

Gene Stevenson

It has not been very long since I joined the team at Indian Bible College (IBC) in Arizona, whose stated mission is "to disciple and educate indigenous Native Christians for lifetimes of biblical ministry and spiritual leadership to their people and the world."[1] One day, shortly into my tenure as academic dean, I confessed to the president of the college that I felt like I was trying to navigate the borderlands between my expertise and my ignorance. Prior to my move to IBC, I had worked hard to cultivate a sense of myself, and had recognized myself as a student, explorer, and reformer. The first two of these ideas run parallel to each other to some extent. A student is someone who explores the world and the limits of his or her knowledge and experience thereof. Such exploration requires an awareness of both the landscapes of knowledge one has already mapped and the unfamiliar landscape to be surveyed. The tools used in this process are tools of observation and listening (first) and then analysis and synthesis (perhaps). These tools have become familiar to me.

Education: a tool of colonization

But the actual history of mostly unhealthy interaction between white Westerners of European descent, such as myself, and Native Americans, our primary constituency at IBC, requires that the synthesis of information be done carefully and any impulse toward reform be deployed gently and only in very specific directions, if at all (in my case thus far, usually in the direction of administrative tasks). Otherwise, a student/explorer can very easily become a parent/conquistador. The legacy of European and Anglo missions work among indigenous people groups—not just in North America, but around the world—shows that this tendency toward paternalism and conquest is a dehumanizing one, often the by-product of a too close relationship between the Church and earthly powers. It must be avoided at all costs.

The need of "border crossings"

As a student, I have learned to lean into what educational theorists call "border crossings": those fish-out-of-water experiences we all have—if we allow ourselves to be open to them—and which serve as signposts for learning.[2] With God's Spirit as my Counselor, my fear of such experiences has largely been quelled, and I have developed an appreciation for those times when I have been introduced to a previously unknown cultural terrain. This allows me in my work as an instructor to reassure my fellow students throughout their experience of a similar process. I may know my area of expertise well and, therefore, be able to help navigate the landmarks that make up that area, but I am also able—and feel compelled—to provide a supportive presence when we together explore areas previously uncharted (for us, anyway).

That's right: teachers are students too! They must be. Because all ignorance is in some sense ignorance of a context, whether that context be historical, cultural, or discipline/field-based. I have spent much of my adult life in and around systems of Western higher education; this is familiar ground to me. But I am still mostly ignorant of the nuances of Native American culture and their diverse tribal expressions. So, my mixture of expertise and ignorance is inverse to that of my students, as it is with anyone involved in cross-cultural ministry. This means that my purpose as an instructor is twofold: 1) to help students become comfortable with having one foot each in the worlds of expertise/knowledge and ignorance, and 2) to guide them through the process of being able to navigate both a First-World, Western society and their own tribal and cultural societies. I am never fully teacher in this process; I am also student. And the students are never fully students; they are also teachers! Here, I follow Jane Vella's lead in considering the learning process as one that takes place "between. . . .learner and learner,"[3] as well as Paulo Freire's, who calls the participants in healthy education "co-investigators."[4]

Subject-based learning

This idea coincides with the theory of subject-based learning, in which the subject—whether Scripture or sentence construction or the scientific method—takes center stage. The subject eclipses both a teacher and student's field of vision and so demands something from both. One of the things it demands from teachers steeped in Western forms of education is that he/she set aside any traditional Western ideas of hierarchy or separation between themselves and their students and recognize that they themselves are students learning alongside other students as the subject is examined.[5] I can share with students what I see and have learned about a subject from my vantage point, even while I invite them to share how they see the subject from their own. This process was fairly natural for me when I taught an anthropology class at IBC; there were entire class periods when I invited the students to teach me about their tribal culture, marriage rituals, and rites of passage, because I honestly did not know about them.

My experience at IBC thus far has taught me this valuable lesson: while my theoretical knowledge compels me to recognize the fact that people's worldviews are shaped from their differing cultural vantage points, my interactions in the classroom have taught me that, actually, at any given moment, multiple overlapping and even contradictory cultural perspectives could be at play within my students. This conclusion has forced me to approach teaching with much more caution than my abstract ideas alone would have demanded, which is ultimately for the good. I have come to recognize the general difference between my white, Western, male perspective and the students' Native American one. But I must go further and recognize that gender, tribal, personal/familial roles, and experience exert an equal (or greater) pull on the minds of the students. It is not out of the ordinary for Native American students, belonging to a specific tribe with its own customs and language to reveal nevertheless that an individualist, Western perspective ruled the day in their upbringing and religious experience. In the end, I as an instructor have been forced to abandon many preconceived and generalized notions of what being a Native American means for my students and must instead listen to their perspectives. A subject-centered approach to teaching facilitates this learning on my part.

Education as re-humanization

For Paulo Freire and other educators based in non-Western cultures, the world—that is, the concrete historical and cultural situations in which people find themselves—is the subject begging to be explored, and this not simply for learning's sake, but for the specific purpose of discovering what about that world prevents learners from living into the God-given opportunity of being fully human. Or, to put it differently, learning is to help remove obstacles to that abundant life which Christ came to give. So, the purpose of such an approach to learning is to "re-humanize" both those who are oppressed and those doing the oppressing (or belonging to the group that has historically oppressed others). If ever a task fits the historical and cultural situation of indigenous people around the world, it is just that.[6] In this case, the words of our brother Dr. Martin Luther King Jr. ring loudly: "Whatever affects one directly, affects all indirectly. I can never be what I ought to be until you are what you ought to be."[7]

Self-giving love

There are many factors that complicate this process. In the wider world of Native America, for instance, Christianity is still very much seen as the "white man's religion." Of course, even Western Christians know this is not true. However, how do we grapple with that prevailing opinion—and even seek to change it—when documented history informs it? This issue is not merely a personal conundrum either. Many IBC students—and other Native Americans—are looked down upon by family and friends because of their faith commitment and/or resulting life choices. Of course, emphasizing the non-Western roots of biblical Christianity is one step toward countering this tendency, because it helps recalibrate the assumptions of those followers of Christ who only know the faith as it has been told by Western voices and shaped by Western culture. And by undermining those expectations, we encourage our indigenous brothers and sisters to be who Christ has made them to be and to articulate the faith in a way that best resonates with their home culture. If we can be humble enough to attempt such acts, they can become signs of self-giving love. But it will take firm knowledge of one's boundaries, trust in God's Spirit who knows the landscape we might be ignorant of, the heart of a student, and a listening ear to hear the perspectives of fellow followers of Christ who do not look or think like we do.

1. www.indianbible.org
2. Ruth Anna Abigail. "By a Crooked Star: Developing Spirituality in the Context of a Faith-Based Institution," in Heewon Chang and Drick Boyd (eds.) *Spirituality in Higher Education: Autoethnographies.* (2011), p.71.
3. Jane Vella. *Learning to Listen, Learning to Teach: The Power of Dialogue in Educating Adults,* Revised. (2002), p.15.
4. Paulo Freire. *Pedagogy of the Oppressed.* (2015), p.106.
5. Parker Palmer. *The Courage to Teach.* (2010), pp.115–117ff.
6. Paulo Freire. *Pedagogy of the Oppressed.* (2015), pp.43ff, 90, 100.
7. Martin Luther King, Jr. *Letter from Birmingham Jail.* (1963).

About Gene Stevenson

Gene led multiple short-term missions teams within the United States during 10 years of service in congregational leadership. He and his wife, Beth, recently moved to Arizona, where Gene has responded to God's call to minister to and with the indigenous North American community in serving as academic dean of Indian Bible College, Flagstaff.

21

A Widow Multiplying
Young Missionaries

Nancy Leatherman

Mission work has been a big part of my life. After serving overseas in various mission assignments with Eastern Mennonite Missions following my college days, my family had been residing in Lancaster County, Pennsylvania, when I was informed that Eastern Mennonite Missions, based in Lancaster, needed a new administrative assistant. What a great delight to be a behind- the-scenes support person to serve a mission organization locally so others could go.

A decade later a friend told me a missions director needed an assistant and recommended I call the office of DOVE Mission International to see how I could help. Peter Bunton, the director, shared what this would involve and I began volunteering. The job included typical office duties: communicating via letters, email, and phone with overseas workers, stateside congregational pastors and leaders, planning meetings and typing notes, plus being a team player with coworkers. However, a new opportunity for youth and missions was about to be launched called Evangelism Missions Training (EMT).

Peter and youth leaders were ready to develop a program to train DOVE youth over several days and then send them in teams on mission assignments whether international or somewhere in the USA or Canada. To plan to send 75–125+ for a training weekend and then get them to their work assignments took plenty of background work. Who would take the responsibility to lead a group of teens to another country? What missionary, national worker, or local church could accept a team? What tasks would be needed—sports outreaches, VBS opportunities, manual labor such as painting or fixing up a building? Evangelism at local parks? How many would their work assignment need? How many could they house and where? Who could guide the youth for their 10-day outreach? Could an interpreter travel with them for the entire assignment? To get answers to these questions and many others took hours of communication. Estimating costs of flights or prices of food, lodging, and fees of rental vans for in-country transportation needed to be decided before we could share the opportunities to the youth group leaders and print literature to be distributed throughout the DOVE network of churches.

Administration to release a new generation of missionaries

For me, a widow in her 60s, I was delighted to help handle these details knowing teenagers and young adults would see their faith increase by joining a team. I knew their relationship with God would deepen. I was aware that trying something new would stretch their self-confidence. Hard work and creative ideas were needed to raise funds so the teenager could participate in EMT.

Do you think mission work necessitates going to another culture or a far-away country, learning a new language, holding evangelistic services in a park, or sharing Bible stories with children? Were just the youth participating in missions or was I also participating in mission work by helping them go? I was delighted to pass along the joy of serving Christ to the younger generation. It brought back many memories of my younger days serving internationally and the challenges I faced and how those experiences brought maturity.

During the 15+ years my husband was a patient in a hospital and I was raising our two children, I couldn't continue our overseas assignment; however, I could be an office worker and send others.

Doing the office tasks was one way I could support missions. Sending rather than going again was a perfect role for me. Providing training opportunities seemed like a logical assignment for me. Of course, senior citizens can "go," retirees can "contribute money," and still others can spend much time "praying" for the youth. But for me during those years, I could make phone calls and send emails to enable the younger generation to experience a mission assignment.

Upon their return from the EMT outreaches, the young people enthusiastically shared their personal stories. My heart would overflow as I listened. They reaped deep joy and contentment from their work. . .and so did I.

About Nancy Leatherman

Nancy served other cultures by teaching at a deaf school in Kingston, Jamaica, and an inner-city school in Philadelphia, PA. She and her late husband served in Belize training young church leaders. After returning to the USA she worked with international students through American Home Life International and as an administrative assistant at Eastern Mennonite Missions, Teaching The Word Ministries, and DOVE Mission International. She is mother of two adult children and grandmother of two.

22

Missions in a Polluted World

Peter Bunton

What do you think of when you hear the term "missions"? Probably many of us think of someone traveling on a plane to another nation to serve the indigenous people. We probably also assume that those people speak a different language and may likely be of a different race to the missionaries who go. In these ways, we usually think of missions as people. They may not know the message of God's love, in which case missionaries preach and proclaim who Christ is. It may be that the people have heard of Christ but need further teaching or discipleship. We probably also imagine people who may be economically poorer than us. Missions in these cases may have a dynamic of educating people with skills to earn a living, or the provision of medical care where there has been little access to medicine. Whatever we envisage, we imagine people. Of course, the above scenarios are often true. Missions focuses on people, and in a sense, so do the Scriptures. We know that the Bible envisions a time when there will be representatives of every tribe and language worshipping in heaven (Revelation 7:9–10).

From providing to supporting sustainability

So, missions is clearly to people. It may require evangelizing people, or discipling people, or serving people in practical capacities through things such as health care and education. Sometimes missions has been giving. This has been particularly true when local needs are great, such as during a time of famine or drought, or where there is a need so large that it would be difficult for the local people to meet that need without external assistance. Especially in times of crisis, giving of finances and other resources may be the appropriate, indeed biblical, thing to do (Acts 11:27–29). Today, however, we are much more aware of matters such as "aid dependency," a dynamic in which both donors feel good about themselves for giving, and receivers continue to expect, perhaps without seeking God's creativity for them to find local solutions to their needs. It has, therefore, become popular to think not of donating (unless in times of severe crisis), but of coming alongside to equip people to flourish in their own lives under God. There is a popular saying along the lines of, "You can give a person a fish and satisfy their hunger today, or you can teach that person to fish so that they will have a livelihood and be able to provide for themselves and their communities on a sustainable basis." Much modern missions, therefore, has focused on skill impartation and even business development.

Impact of broader societal issues on missions

While the above is good, we may find that our laudable emphasis on reaching individuals or small groups for discipleship and training may lead to some frustrations. For example, "It's better to teach a person to fish than to give him or her a fish" may seem a truism. Yet, what happens if the multinational industrial complex upriver is polluting the water with its by-products? The infusion of chemicals and waste may pollute the environment, killing wildlife. Indeed, there may no longer be any fish to be caught!

Shalom: a goal of missions

This can become a huge challenge to us when doing missions. Indeed, what is the point of training people for livelihoods which cannot function because of larger structural, environmental, or political issues? This then causes many in missions to freak out! Yes, I just mentioned the word "political," which sends many Christians running. Indeed, we are often told that the Church should not be political. For the missionary, however, not to engage the broader societal issues of industrial pollution means the missionary project to help people extricate themselves from poverty is doomed to failure. The missionary who has gone to tell individuals about Jesus and focus on their personal needs may find that missions is now about broader social engagement. Can this still be missions? It certainly is not what most of us think of, as illustrated in the first paragraph. To answer this question, maybe we have to return to the beginning and ask ourselves, "What is the purpose of missions?" Yes, it is important to preach Christ; yes, it is important to evangelize; yes, it is important to engage in personal discipleship. However, the goal of missions, as articulated by Christ in Matthew 28:18–20, is to make the *nations*, not just individuals, disciples of Christ. How then do we make a whole nation or people a disciple of Christ? Surely, it is not simply to evangelize individuals, but it is so that the believers in that nation will work to see every aspect of their national life become submitted to God and glorify Him. This means that businesses must be righteous and ethical; it means that art and mass media should be committed to truth; it means that laws and regulations should be just and administered justly so that all citizens have the opportunity to flourish spiritually, physically, emotionally, and relationally. Indeed, this is what the Old Testament Scriptures call *shalom*. This concept has been defined by the theologian Cornelius Plantinga simply as "the way things are supposed to be."[1] If *shalom*—a society fully glorifying God—is the goal, then it does become appropriate for our missions to engage the structural issues in communities which keep people impoverished, unhealthy, and not leading the abundant life Jesus desires.

Community transformation

So, missions is entirely personal, as God takes an interest in each one of us. We have also seen, however, that it may move beyond the individual and personal to be a prophetic proclamation to the very structures of society. This becomes permissible if we see the goal of missions as not simply people acknowledging Christ or church planting, but we envision the compelling vision of *shalom* on the earth. We are motivated by the desire that God would receive glory in every area of a society, and further compelled to serve all peoples, knowing that each of us is made in God's image (Genesis 1:26–27) and is thus worthy of dignity. Those who bear God's image are not just to survive, but flourish on this earth, just as the Lord intended (Genesis 1:29–30; 2:15). Yes, missions is personal, but it is also to transform communities and whole societies.

1. Cornelius Plantinga. "Sin: Not the way it's supposed to be". (2010), p.3. Available at: http://tgc-documents.s3.amazonaws.com/cci/Pantinga.pdf.

About Peter Bunton

Peter, originally from Great Britain, lives in Pennsylvania. His main responsibility is the director of DOVE Mission International, where he helps develop and send missionaries from the USA. He received a PhD in missiology from the University of Manchester, England, for his research in founders' succession in international Christian movements and organizations.

23

Giving What We Cannot Keep to Gain What We Cannot Lose

Nancy Barnett

"He is no fool who gives what he cannot keep to gain what he cannot lose," penned Jim Elliot, one of the more well-known martyrs for Christ of our modern age.

As a teenager, I read the amazing story of how Jim and his coworkers were killed by the Auca Indians they were trying to reach with the message and love of Christ and how his wife and toddler returned to live with this tribe.

My friends who paid the ultimate price

Of course, I never knew Jim Elliot. But I did know Tom Little, David Goodman, and JS. Men whose faces come to my mind this morning as I reflect on today, designated the International Day of the Christian Martyr. Men whose blood spilled on the soil of the lands they had adopted as their own.

I met Tom and his wife, Libbie, while attending a school in the Netherlands back in the seventies. They were preparing to move to Afghanistan. I remember their sweet toddler and the joy their family brought to our group of predominately singles. I lost track of them after that. And then, ten years ago, a mobile medical team in a remote village of Afghanistan was killed by the Taliban. My heart sank when I saw his name on that list.

Later I read an interview with his wife and learned what had transpired since those long-ago days in the Netherlands. They now had three daughters who had grown up in war-torn Afghanistan: "We raised our three daughters through what was, at times, just hell. A hundred rockets a day was a good day." Family members lived underground to avoid bombings. Yet they stayed out of a love for the people and a passion for providing health care to the needy. Their compelling passion was to share the love of Jesus. Spending so many years there wasn't their original plan, but Libbie spoke of how, as a young couple, they had committed their lives to serve God together; once they arrived in Afghanistan, they simply fell in love with the people. Seeing the overwhelming need of the poor without medical care drew them to make this nation their home and life's calling.

David and Jenny Goodman were a couple my husband, Tom, and I had met as singles traveling on a short-term mission team in Turkey. They welcomed us into their home, making our stay with them probably the highlight of my time there. I was deeply impacted by the love they had for the Turkish people even though building relationships was a slow and arduous process. A year after our visit with them, I opened the newspaper one day and was stunned to read of David's death. I learned later that he was having his devotions in his home one morning, when he answered the door and was shot point blank by a gunman. His wife was eight months pregnant with their first child.

My relationship with JS was much more familiar since he grew up in the church we pastored. We watched him go off to college, have a transformational faith encounter, meet his wife, and pursue missionary training. Years later, we gathered as a church family to pray and bless their family (which now included a son) as they left for the Arabian Peninsula. Ten years ago, Tom and I had the privilege of visiting them there and experiencing a small taste of the lifestyle they had embraced. In their short time, J had already displayed an amazing grasp of the Arabic language and, together with some teammates, had been offered leadership of a vocational training institute. In a land where women's faces are always veiled, his wife, JA, opened her home for tea and friendship, continued with rigorous language studies, and learned to navigate driving in a city where almost all rules are ignored. Quite honestly, I was in awe of them as I witnessed first-hand their courageous faith and sacrificial lifestyle.

And then came the 3:00 a.m. call one Sunday morning in March of 2012. JS had been gunned down in his car, targeted by Al Qaeda. I will never forget how our church gathered for worship just a few hours later in our stunned disbelief. Never have I experienced a Sunday like that one where we came together and simply wept. We held each other and worshipped the best we could through an abundance of tears.

JA and her boys returned to Pennsylvania. We continued to marvel at the courage and faith of this godly young woman and her children (as well as JS's parents and siblings) as we watched them on this new journey of grief. In the years since, JA has remarried and a precious daughter has been added to their family. We continue to hear of amazing things happening in this war- and poverty-stricken land—life coming from that seed that went into the ground and died.

It has been said that "the blood of the martyrs is the seed of the Church." As I sit here on a Monday morning in the comfort of my home, I think of the many around the world who are willingly laying down their lives so that others will know the love of Jesus. Some have paid the ultimate price, having given what they could not keep to gain what they will never lose.

About Nancy Barnett

Nancy and her husband, Tom, met as "YWAMers" (Youth With A Mission) in Spain where they lived for 12 years. They have pastored DOVE Christian Fellowship Elizabethtown since 1994 and know the joy of releasing many of their members (including their own children) to serve around the world. Nancy is a trained spiritual director and enjoys listening to and encouraging others in their faith journey.

24

Wide-Eyed Wonder and Raw Humanity

God's Love for Those with Special Needs

Elizabeth Vanderhorst

Like a string of Polaroid pictures, moment after moment floods my mind. The impact of special needs people in my life has been vast.

Special needs and wonderful encounters

Mr. Chris made me nervous. He was intellectually disabled, and I, as a young girl of 6 or 7 years old, didn't know much about special needs. All I knew was that this guy helping out at church always wanted to give me a high five. So even though special needs scared me, I would give him a high five and a smile and then quickly hide. I haven't seen him in almost 20 years and have come a long way in my understanding of people with special needs, but do you know what I remember most about Mr. Chris? His smile. He was always smiling and kind to the people around him.

I felt rough hands grab my neck and shoulders as he came up behind me for a hug. "*Suave, Suave!*" ("Gentle, Gentle!") I said to the teenage boy who was so excited to have visitors at his orphanage in Peru. We helped channel some of his excited energy as we played ball in the yard with a ball made from a plastic bread bag and plant stems shoved inside. He had a huge grin on his face the entire time.

Tears fill my eyes every year at Night to Shine Prom. As Audio Adrenaline's song "Kings & Queens" plays over the loudspeaker, *"Boys become kings / Girls will be queens / Wrapped in Your majesty / When we love, when we love the least of these,"* people with special needs walk down the red carpet in their handsome suits and beautiful dresses to be crowned the king and queen of the ball. They dance with their buddies and take silly pictures in the photobooth. The pure joy of the night is indescribable as we dance and celebrate the worth of humans!

In Medellín, Colombia, we took a suitcase of craft supplies and activities and wheeled it to one of the schools for special needs people. There I guided the hands of a blind lady to complete a craft. Our team laughed and watched our new friends who were deaf sign quickly to each other and we played baseball and painted nails.

I had the privilege of dancing at my wedding with my friend Brittani, while my new groom supported Brittani as she stood and danced with me. You see, Brittani has spina bifida and is in a wheelchair, and lack of feeling in her legs and general leg weakness make it difficult for her to stand for long periods of time. But I promised her that if she worked hard in physical therapy, we would find a way to dance standing up at my wedding—we did, and we have the pictures to prove it!

The other day I ran into the grocery store and I could tell that the man talking to the cashier had special needs. He and I made eye contact as we packed our groceries and said "Hello!" The man who was with my new friend remarked to him, "You must be a regular here, knowing all these people." My new friend turned to me and said, "Have we met before?" I responded that I didn't think so, but that he seemed like a friendly guy so I thought I would be friendly back. He said, "Oh, I am a nice guy!" I laughed and agreed. As he left the store, he turned to me and held his hand out for a fist bump, which I gladly gave, before leaving with the biggest smile under my mask.

During the coronavirus lockdown of 2020, my husband and I went for a walk at a local park. We didn't pass many people, but towards the end of our walk, we passed a mom and her teenaged daughter with special needs. I smiled at them and all of a sudden, the girl came over and gave me a huge hug. Her mom said, "I'm sorry, I've been trying to teach her about social distancing, but it's hard." I laughed and said it was fine. I wasn't bothered; I was delighted.

The world is full of people waiting to be loved

I mention all these moments to show that no matter where we are in life, physically or metaphorically, there are encounters to be had. The variety of special needs and what they look like is a broad category—it may be a physical, emotional, or intellectual disability, it may be visible or invisible to outsiders, it may affect daily life a lot or not much at all, it may be congenital or acquired. The world is full of people waiting to be loved.

Jesus served those with special needs

Someone else had a lot of encounters with people, a lot of whom had special needs. Jesus. Matthew chapters 8 through 12 are full of daily encounters that Jesus had with people who had special needs. People with leprosy, infectious diseases, and stigma (8:1–4). Demon-possessed people (8:16, 28–34). Paralyzed people (9:1–8). People with bleeding and blood disorders (9:18–26). Blind people (9:27–31). People unable to speak (9:32–34). People with hand deformities (12:9–14). People with epilepsy and disorders of the mind (17:15). In a crowd of people, Jesus saw them. Not only did He see them, he also pulled them into the center of attention with Him.

In the play *Jesus* at Sight & Sound Theater in Lancaster, Pennsylvania, I love the scene where Jesus heals the man with leprosy. He puts his hands on the face of the man, heals him, and then proceeds to turn to his horrified disciples and touch them with the same hands. It's shocking and profound. He does the same thing in our lives, He says, "These are my people; love them." No ifs, ands, or buts. No qualifications required on our part or their part.

Special needs people are a gift. Much like the disciples, we don't always know how to embrace people that can be seen as fringe people or outcasts. We worry we will mess it up so we do nothing. Start somewhere. Smile, engage, ask questions, say "hi." We can learn many lessons from special needs people, but two of the biggest ones are wide-eyed wonder (also known as childlike faith) and raw humanity.

Wide-eyed wonder

"Learn this well: Unless you dramatically change your way of thinking and become teachable, and learn about heaven's kingdom realm with the wide-eyed wonder of a child, you will never be able to enter in" Matthew 18:3 (TPT).

Wide-eyed wonder is what we get when we notice small details like the petals of a flower or the texture of tree bark. It's what we get when we experience life through the eyes of an innocent person. We learn wide-eyed wonder when we create margin in our schedules for encounters with people and then the encounters actually happen. Wide-eyed wonder appears when we learn how to celebrate the smallest victories. When we learn wide-eyed wonder in our daily lives, it spills over into our faith and the way we view our relationship with God.

Have you ever met a person with Down syndrome? Their beautiful slanted eyes are often accompanied with a wide smile, a tenacious personality, and joy. One of my Down syndrome students serenaded me with a rousing rendition of "Happy Birthday" using a toy guitar during a Zoom therapy session the other day. Even though it wasn't my birthday, they were insistent on wanting to sing to me. I can't help but smile when I'm in the presence of people with Down syndrome because they teach me so much about joy and wonder.

Being with people who have special needs, especially cognitive impairments, invites us to embrace wonder, simplicity, and childlike faith. It gives us a fresh perspective on things that we have hardened our hearts towards and replaces cynicism.

Raw humanity

"O Lord, our Lord,
how majestic is your name in all the earth!
You have set your glory above the heavens.
Out of the mouth of babies and infants,
you have established strength because of your foes,
to still the enemy and the avenger.
When I look at your heavens, the work of your fingers,
the moon and the stars, which you have set in place,
what is man that you are mindful of him,
and the son of man that you care for him?"

Psalm 8:1–4 (ESV)

Being around people with special needs reveals a layer of raw humanity that we often try to forget about. Like the oozing sores of the leper as he walked towards Jesus, or the friends of the paralytic who lowered him through a roof to see Jesus, or when Jesus mixed spit and dirt to place mud on the blind man's eye, we tend to push these things aside as unpleasant occurrences. When you are a caregiver for someone, you often do a lot of tasks (depending on what the need is) that aren't what you would pick—toileting them, showering them, having discussions about hygiene, giving grace with and teaching social skills, having the same conversation repeatedly if they have dementia or short-term memory loss—and you must do the tasks with humility and kindness. The topic of body fluids makes most of us a little squeamish. Yet, what if these are the moments that grace and peace flood into the most?

The psalms are full of raw humanity. David (and the other psalm-writers) felt all sorts of emotions that we wrestle with on a daily basis: anger, depression, helplessness, happiness, gratitude, frustration, impatience, jealousy.

Being around special needs people often reveals raw humanity out of necessity, but what if it is exactly what we need to practice vulnerability? Life and circumstances aren't usually pretty and tied up in bows of conclusions; they are messy and raw and real. When we face things head on, that's where lives change.

1 Corinthians 9:19–23 (The Message) states, "Even though I am free of the demands and expectations of everyone, I have voluntarily become a servant to any and all in order to reach a wide range of people: religious, nonreligious, meticulous moralists, loose-living immoralists, the defeated, the demoralized—whoever. I didn't take on their way of life. I kept my bearings in Christ—but I entered their world and tried to experience things from their point of view. I've become just about every sort of servant there is in my attempts to lead those I meet into a God-saved life. I did all this because of the Message. I didn't just want to talk about it; I wanted to be in on it!"

We all have special needs

We all have special needs of some type—let us use them to draw us closer to God and each other. Instead of being afraid of what we don't know, let us be kind and caring. Let us not look on people with pity, but on what they teach us about the character of Christ. Let us be willing to hold on tightly to wide-eyed wonder and raw humanity as we do the work of the gospel here on earth. God's heart for missions includes all people.

About Elizabeth Vanderhorst

Elizabeth has co-led missions teams to Ireland and Colombia. In addition, she has served on teams to Alaska and Georgia. Elizabeth volunteers every summer at a camp for foster children. She loves people and seeing what God is doing in hearts all around the world.

25

Starting a Business in a Creative Access Nation

R & M

When you think of a missionary, what do you imagine their day-to-day looks like? Bible studies, street evangelism, organizing mercy ministries in the community? Do you picture them running a business? Maybe a gym? Or as a wedding planner? Or a web designer?

You've probably heard about countries where it's against the law to convert to Christianity. Places in the Middle East, parts of Africa, southeast Asia, and so on. In these countries where proselytizing itself is illegal, governments are obviously not handing out missionary visas. In fact, they are carefully scrutinizing those applying for residency. So how do missionaries find legal ways to live in these places? How do we "go into all the world" when parts of the world are "closed?"

No place is closed to God

First of all, no place is closed to the gospel. As hard as it can be to gain access to some countries, no country is truly closed. There is always a way; you just have to be creative. That's why we prefer to call these places "creative access" rather than "closed" countries. You can go as a student, employee, retiree, NGO worker, or you can start your own business.

Opening up a business in a creative access nation offers not only a solid identity, but also creates many opportunities within the community. When we moved to a creative access nation we started our own media business. All of the businesses we mentioned in the beginning—gym owners, web designers, wedding planners—are ones that missionaries in creative access nations can start in order to gain access into that country.

Integrity

As followers of Christ, if we are going to go this route, then we should do it with full integrity. This means that if we say we are web designers, then we should design websites. If we run a business, we should run it with excellence and not merely use it as a cover for other work. This wouldn't model a good work ethic and integrity to our fellow believers and the nationals around us.

Running your own business also brings the opportunity to hire nationals to work alongside you. This provides not only employment but the opportunity to do life with someone day to day. We've had this opportunity in our own business. This provided us with so many open doors for sharing the gospel and also modelled what it means to follow Jesus, even when we do so imperfectly. Additionally, it opens doors to connect with clients and other people in your field. We know many who operate language centers in creative access countries. The constant interaction and discussions with students have offered so many open doors for discussions, relationships, and even starting Bible studies with interested students.

Running a business can propel missionaries into the heart of a community. And practically speaking, it helps people to understand how and why you're in their community.

Before we make it sound like running a business in a creative access nation is a silver bullet, we would caution that running a business is not for everyone—and it requires a lot of work! Imagine all of the challenges of starting a business in your home country—marketing, taxes, accounting, daily operations, etc. Now try doing that in a country with laws very different from those you're familiar with (and often vague and open to a variety of interpretations). These difficulties are compounded by it all being in a foreign language, and in a culture very different than your own.

It is hard work running a business, and not all businesses will thrust you into community or daily interactions with nationals. On top of running a business, you will need to make time for language learning and being in the community meeting people.

There are a few other ways to do business in a creative access nation. You can be hired by a national company and receive a visa through them. This also provides consistent income (which running your own business does not!) and a higher level of identity. However, you have less flexibility and freedom. Some of these type of jobs also require long work hours and may leave little time for connecting in your community.

Another option is to be hired by a like-minded worker who has already started a company. In this scenario it's much easier to get a visa, you're not responsible for every aspect of the business, and there's generally more flexibility because you're both ultimately in the country for the same reasons. However, too many foreigners working in the same business (particularly if the business isn't bringing in much income) can raise suspicion. It's also important to take into account who you go into business with and have very clearly defined expectations and everything put into writing.

Business can be part of every nation being transformed by God

Doing business as missions has its share of challenges, but we praise God that there are viable options for living in creative access nations with full integrity. We need to continue finding creative ways of residing in these places so that we can be a part of seeing every nation and tribe reached with the transforming news of the gospel.

About R & M

R & M are workers in a creative access nation.

26

Reaching Unchurched Youth in South Africa

Joel Smucker

Do you want to change the world for the better? Do you want others to embrace the message of Christ and make a far greater impact than you have? A key way to do this is to invest in the younger generation. They are tomorrow's leaders and are the most impressionable and reachable.

My wife, Marion, and I started reaching out to youth in Cape Town, South Africa, four years ago. We had moved from the USA and teamed up with a church which asked us to be youth leaders. There were only a few youth in the church, but the community had kids running around the streets. We chose to include those "unchurched" kids in our program. Some came from difficult personal or living situations such as being HIV+ or being surrounded and influenced by drugs and gangsterism. Some came from stable family homes, but they were an exception. However, no matter what a person's situation in life, we all need Jesus. Children and youth are no exception. Whether you are reaching the poorest of the poor or the extremely wealthy, reaching them for Christ will make an eternal difference.

Youth leading other youth

We have seen many kids come and go for various reasons, and we have realized that our energy and resources are not limitless.

For that reason, even though we make ourselves available to all, we spend the most energy on the ones that receive the message of the gospel and are the most apt to share with someone else. One of the biggest breakthroughs we saw was when two girls in the youth group were filled with the Holy Spirit and started ministering to the other youth. In the beginning of that year, the junior youth group was not going well because many in the group were disruptive and argumentative. We were considering dropping that part of the youth group because it didn't seem to be going anywhere. The two girls, however, asked to help teach the younger kids. Through their influence a revival happened with the younger group. They learned to worship the Lord and pray for each other. On more than one occasion they would lead the group by themselves. Afterward, we would show up and find them all weeping and praying in the presence of God. It was then that we realized that maybe part of our purpose was to create a space for these young people to lead the revival themselves. I really think that other youth are the best people to reach the younger generation.

Love and genuine relationship

We have discovered that there are two crucial matters when working with youth: be genuine and love them. You can have the most sophisticated and best-funded programs to better the lives of youth, but what really grabs their attention is a genuine relationship with role models who care about them.

Creative outreach strategies

When reaching kids who are not used to church, we sometimes have to use a creative approach. The goal is not necessarily to bring them into our churches but to introduce them to Christ. Our church model is not itself a gospel imperative, and it may or may not be effective with the group we are reaching. It is, therefore, sometimes necessary to do things differently in order to "become all things to all men so that we might win some to Christ." As long as the gospel message we preach is pure and we reach out to them with the love of God, the nuts and bolts of how things are done are very negotiable; we should use whatever is effective. You might find a common interest to gather people. You could use soccer, for example, or anything that you can use as a reason to gather. Then through the relationships that develop, you can share the gospel and love of Jesus Christ. When a few of them decide to follow Christ and become disciples, it may be a good time to introduce them to your church, or it may work best to simply call whatever platform that brought you together your new church.

Youth work: unpredictable but worth it!

Working with kids can be very unpredictable. Sometimes you may spend years investing in a child, and suddenly his parents decide to move to another neighborhood: you never see him again. At other times, when a young person transitions to high school and experiences developmental changes, you may find that you transitioned from being his favorite person to his boring, old-fashioned former youth leader! It is important to serve unselfishly, expecting nothing in return, other than the hope that your investment in their life will have a lifelong impact and help make that person the best they can be in life. Sometimes, they might thank you, but most of the time they will not see the extent of your sacrifice until much later in life. However, God sees. If you truly love the people He has asked you to serve, your greatest joy will be to see them thrive, regardless of whether you get any recognition or not. We have a friend who grew up in a Muslim family. When she attended a church youth group in her neighborhood, she gave her life to Christ. Since she was still living with her parents, she never told anyone about the commitment she had made to Christ, and continued living the Muslim life. However, when she came of age she went public with her faith. She and her husband then went on to start a church in their neighborhood.

Never forget the importance and value of the seeds of the gospel that we plant in the minds of young children and youth. We may plant the seed, we may water the new growth, but it is God who makes the plant grow and brings it to fruition.

About Joel Smucker

Joel and Marion, from the USA and Kenya respectively, spent time in South Africa, where Joel served as a pastor. After a period of living in the USA, they felt the Lord calling them and their children to return to ministry in the Cape Town area of South Africa. They currently work with youth in House of Praise and also lead a cycle club that Joel started to reach the teenage boys who were unchurched, and indeed did not like church. They serve on the eldership team of House of Praise, a DOVE church in Woodstock, South Africa.

27

A Mission of Making Peace in a Conflict-Ridden World

Kellie Swope

> Blessed are the peacemakers,
> for they shall be called sons of God.
>
> Matthew 5:9 (ESV)

Two weeks ago, I had a dream. I was far in the future and I realized there were no birds. In the way of dreams, I produced a bird that I had brought with me from the past, and people gathered around me, marveling at its beautiful melody because they had never heard a bird song.

I dreamt this on the week I was preparing a message for a Sunday service about peacemakers. I realized if we do not do something now, the song of the peacemaker could be lost to future generations.

Peacemaker: an identifying characteristic of a disciple of Christ

"When Jesus saw the crowds, He went up on the mountain; and after He sat down, His disciples came to Him. He opened His mouth and began to teach them, saying. . ." (Matthew 5:1–2, New American Standard Bible).

Jesus preached the famous Sermon on the Mount not to huge crowds like many assume, but to his disciples. The things He spoke to them in Matthew 5, 6, and 7 were of such vital importance that they would become markers of followers of Christ. In these chapters we find exactly what Jesus wanted His disciples to become to prepare them for the trials of persecution they would face soon. Tucked away in Matthew 5 is a message to the peacemakers. Verse 9 says, "*Blessed are the peacemakers*, for they shall be called sons of God" (ESV, emphasis mine). Here Jesus is saying *peacemaking* is our identity. The ability to make peace is an identifying marker indicating us as children of God. Why is that so? Because God Himself is a peacemaker. As children of God we take after our Father in heaven! When we become peacemakers, we are acting so much like God that people identify us as His children. Even if others do not, certainly God Himself sees us as such.

Christ as a peacemaker

The truth is He Himself is a peacemaker and a reconciler. Whether through healing and deliverance, revealing truth to His followers, or—yes—even through flipping tables and the minds of the religious who opposed him, Jesus' mission on earth was all about making peace between God and man. And let us not forget that the most important peace that Christ brokered was the peace He made for us so that *we* can have peace with our creator.

So, what does it mean to be a peacemaker? I can tell you what it is not. It is not being a *peacekeeper*, if that means being one who remains silent just to avoid disagreement when an honest discussion of differences may be needed. This would be a person who will tell someone what they think they want to hear even if their heart and actions in secret do not agree. To put it plainly: *peacekeepers* in this sense are liars. This kind of peacekeeping is not *making* peace. To make peace between people and groups of people, you must find the courage to be honest and to have enough self-control to let the other person speak without dismissing them or defending your point. I admit I still fail at this at times, especially when others oppose a belief I hold to be truth from Scripture.

Church with refugees and asylum seekers

As part of my mission in Germany, I provide a place of emotional healing to refugees from war-torn countries and who have lived under the thumb of oppressive regimes. Refugees crossing borders is a hot-button issue. People of one narrative see them as potential usurpers of the beliefs and rights they hold dear. People of another see it as a humanitarian issue that needs to be addressed. How do I as a peacemaker address and make peace between, at times, two very opposing ideologies to get people on board with God's mission? I'm still trying to work that out. I have found that one helpful thing is to get people to listen to the stories of others. Listening to the heart of people and making space for them to share honestly is key in any peacemaking strategy.

Here in Germany we have refugees who have joined our church who are all in different stages of the immigration process. We provide aid in this process, but during the long wait for court appointments and immigration office appointments, they join us in home groups and various other forms of fellowship. One of our favorite things to share—besides food, of course—are discussions of the differences in the cultures in which we grew up. Many in our groups come from warm culture countries where people are smiling and friendly, but consider it rude to speak in a direct manner or cut each other off for sake of time. However, they have come to a culture where indirectness seems suspicious and untrustworthy; efficiency is something to value, including being *pünktlich*—on the dot, timewise.

The difference of ways in which direct and indirect culture interacts can easily lead to misinterpreting each other's motivations. We have found that when it's talked about openly, the misunderstandings are far fewer and it's more likely that they will respect each other's boundaries. Neither is asking it of each other; it just becomes natural because of the love that is already sown through the help that has been given. In fact, you can almost see the light bulb turn on when people see the whys behind the other culture's behavior and that the behavior most likely had nothing to do with rudeness or sneakiness. It is simply due to how they were raised to behave in their culture. The only way to realize this, however, is by talking about it face to face and bringing it out in the open.

I had no idea when I first started working with Persian people the potential for insult I would give, just by being a woman raised in America. This is not due to American ideology or what they had heard about us in Iran, but because I warmly greet people I consider brothers and sisters in Christ! I quickly realized my way of greeting caused a dilemma for my new friends who came from backgrounds of restricted interactions between men and women. Some felt uncomfortable, but they did not want to offend by telling me directly. When I realized something was amiss by their reactions, I, quite directly for an American raised in Lancaster County, Pennsylvania, asked them what would be considered an appropriate greeting between friends in their culture. The discussion that ensued was so helpful. I have to give my sweet, Persian friends credit for not giving up on me because I might have crossed boundaries and been too ignorant of their ways. In the end, the stalwart German handshake became the compromise (at least in pre-COVID-19 days), and relationships were deepened by having meals together to facilitate the discussion, all buffered by much laughter and love.

Don't get offended; make peace

To be a peacemaker, we must not easily be offended. That is why it's so important to allow God to work *in us* before we seek change in others. Don't get me wrong—my Persian friends were willing to change. They told me that they had after all come to another country and culture, not the other way around. When they saw how interested we were in living in peace with them by learning about their culture, it drew people to the message of Christ.

As Christians we should be known as people who bring respite to a conflict-ridden world, not ones who fuel conflict. Just like the birds missing in the dream I had of the future, the world is increasingly losing the song of the peacemakers. We need to learn how to be sons and daughters of God by making peace in the name of Christ even though we have failed in ancient church history, in recent church history, and where we are failing even now.

> Lord, make me an instrument of your peace:
> where there is hatred, let me sow love;
> where there is injury, pardon;
> where there is doubt, faith;
> where there is despair, hope;
> where there is darkness, light;
> where there is sadness, joy.
>
> O divine Master,
> grant that I may not so much seek
> to be consoled as to console,
> to be understood as to understand,
> to be loved as to love.
> For it is in giving that we receive,
> it is in pardoning that we are pardoned,
> and it is in dying that we are born to eternal life.
> Amen.
>
> Peace Prayer of Saint Francis

About Kellie Swope

A graduate of Morningstar School of Ministry and co-founder of Isaiah 61 Freedom Ministries, Kellie has served as a missionary from DOVE Westgate Church since 2018. She ministers to people from persecuted church areas of the world displaced in eastern Germany. She is on the leadership team of her local church in Germany where she disciples new believers and works in all aspects of church life.

28

Missions: Fulfilling the Father's Dreams and Desires

Bill Landis

The Father's dreams for the nations

Our Father, the maker of heaven and earth, has dreams and desires for every nation, tribe, tongue, family, and individual! Missions is being close enough to our Father God so that we begin to feel and understand His heart's desire to reveal Himself to a particular people and place. Another way of saying it is to be close enough that the Holy Spirit reveals what is breaking the Father's heart. In the past few years my wife, Val, and I discovered that there had not been a public proclamation of the gospel in the nation of Barbados for many years. We realized that the Father's desire was that the next generation would have a chance to hear the good news. This led us to begin to pray for a new wave of evangelism. Out of these prayer times we formed partnerships with local believers and performing arts evangelism teams. The gospel was proclaimed in more than 100 schools and public sports fields; over 100,000 people heard the good news! The Scriptures declare the dreams of our Father and His Son, Jesus to fill the earth with knowledge of His glory, and that it is not the desire of the Father that any should perish but that all would come to knowledge of salvation. There are so many unfulfilled dreams that the Father has. He is looking for sons and daughters to want to be around Him. When you are around someone, you become close to them.

You begin to know what brings them joy and what makes them sad. Jesus said He came to restore us to the Father; Jesus said He only does and says what He sees the Father doing and saying. Jesus sent the Holy Spirit to fill us with this ability to know the Father's will and to have the power to do the Father's will.

Missions requires a relationship with the Holy Spirit

To engage in missions is also to be dependent on our relationship with the Holy Spirit. It is amazing that while Jesus was on earth, He repeatedly said He was the Son of Man. He came in the form of a man, filled with the Holy Spirit! Everything Jesus did on earth was as a man filled with the Holy Spirit. When Jesus ascended, He sent this same Holy Spirit to enable us to do the works He was doing.

Missions is dependent on risks of faith

A third point of understanding missions is the requirement that we take risks of faith. Nothing in the Kingdom happens without a risk of faith! Our Father and His Son, Jesus, will reveal by the Holy Spirit what His dream, desire, and will is. We respond with "Yes! You, Father, and you, King Jesus, are able to do this!" We respond with faith, then we listen for simple instructions which we obey (acts of faith). We stay engaged, contending for this desire, and obey His simple instructions until the Father fulfills His word. We do the 1%, and He does the 99%. This happened with the birthing of Caribbean Prayer Rooms. A few years ago, a colleague and I were driving down the road in Kansas City. The Holy Spirit filled our car and we heard the Father's desire to have night and day prayer from the islands of the Caribbean. We said, "Yes, Father, you are able to do this." We had no clue how, but we said "yes." As we began to pray for prayer rooms to come into existence, we felt a call to move to Barbados and build on a prayer initiative that had become dormant. The new effort led first to a Caribbean Prayer Room beginning at YWAM Barbados; we were then instructed to have an annual gathering which led to around eight new prayer rooms starting in other Caribbean nations. Each year the leaders of these continue to gather to encourage one another and to allow the Holy Spirit to teach us.

In summary, let's get close to our Father so we know His heart for people and places. Let's be sensitive to the Holy Spirit so that we know what to do today and tomorrow and take risks of faith to see our Father's dreams and desires fulfilled in the earth in our generation.

About Bill Landis

Bill and his wife, Val, have served with Youth With A Mission (YWAM) for over 30 years. They pioneered and led three YWAM ministry locations: Grenada, Barbados, and Montego Bay, Jamaica. They have launched teams to pioneer ministries in places such as Trinidad & Tobago, Albania, and the Gambia. Bill and Val now live in Lancaster, PA, and serve with YWAM Lancaster as senior elders and as senior elders of YWAM Caribbean. Bill and Val have three grown children, all of whom are married, and they have five delightful grandchildren.

29

Reconciliation between Peoples and Nations

Dave Smith

Christian missions today may look different than it did 2,000 years ago, but the goal remains the same: fulfilling the Great Commission. The means of achieving that mission, however, are different. Many of the unreached areas our predecessors traveled to are now the areas where Christianity is growing the fastest. As cross-cultural missions have spread, important questions have arisen, such as, "Do I have to worship God in the same ways as the foreign missionaries do?" Just as we have encountered denominational differences in the Western world, similar differences have arisen in the more recently evangelized areas. Baptism methods, worship styles, which cultural practices are viewed as wrong have all been debated. Such issues have created mistrust with the subsequent need for reconciliation—between cultures, ministries, and reconciliation with their heavenly Father.

In Romans 11:15 (The Amplified Bible), Paul writes, "For if their [present] rejection [of salvation] is for the reconciliation of the world [to God], what will their acceptance [of salvation] be but [nothing less than] life from the dead?" Paul, a Jewish Roman citizen, is communicating to the early Gentile church how God had graciously grafted in and allowed the Gentiles into the promises of the Abrahamic covenant through the sacrifice of Jesus Christ. More simply put, Israel was God's chosen people, but God brought the opportunity for all peoples to be reconciled with God through Jesus. The dictionary defines "reconciliation" as "the action of making one view or belief compatible with another." This emphasizes reconciliation as *action*, not just words.

When reconciliation became necessary, possible, and attainable

When Adam and Eve first ate the fruit of the tree of knowledge of good and evil, a separation occurred between God and His children. There was a desire in both heaven and Earth for this separation to be restored. In the story of the tower of Babel in Genesis 11, humans in their arrogance believed they could solve this problem by connecting to God in their own strength. God hindered such plans and caused them to speak different languages.

How could God be so mean? Think about how much language influences culture. Words and songs reflect much of what we see. In some cultures, the beat of songs makes us want to move, and their words are often very descriptive. Imagine that perhaps God wasn't being mean, but instead was allowing the human race to develop different cultures. Different aspects of culture enable us to see and share such different aspects of who God is, such as through language and art. God knew that humans could never enter His presence merely on their own. Perhaps, though, they could know Him more through His creation and the cultures they would develop.

Ultimately, Jesus' crucifixion, resurrection, and the gift of the Holy Spirit would make it possible for humans to reconcile with God once again. After Jesus ascended to heaven, the disciples experienced Pentecost. As the Holy Spirit came upon them, they began speaking in different languages and proclaiming what Jesus had done. This was a redemption of the tower of Babel. Where once the human race had tried (and failed) to reconcile to God on their own, now God had made way to do this through His Son! Not only that, but He was communicating to them in the very languages He had caused them to speak all those years earlier!

He was bringing understanding where confusion once had been, and made it accessible to everyone, not just the Jews.

How does all of this relate to missions?

In Matthew 28:18–20 and elsewhere, Jesus commissions us to make all peoples His disciples, and to proclaim that Jesus is the way to relationship with Father God. For the last 2,000 years, many Christians have tried to reconcile people to God. Like most things, however, the process isn't always easy. To use an analogy of marriage, two people come together and quickly learn they have different understandings of their roles within the family, finances, and expectations. Indeed, disagreements may get so serious that God is needed to bring the couple to unity as they regroup around His values and principles. Occasionally there are significant issues that surface in a marriage, causing more than just a disagreement. Things like adultery and broken trust can cause separation and hurt in a relationship. In this case, words are often not enough to bridge the gap. An action is required as well. For example, if a spouse commits adultery, asking for forgiveness is a first step, but additional actions are needed, such as an accountability process to provide grounds to trust again.

Similarly, in cross-cultural missions, two very diverse cultures are coming together over one concept. Trust needs to be built and can be very fragile at the beginning. While many have come to Christ through missions, there have often been misunderstandings, with missionaries seeking to impose their own culture on others. Missiologist Paul Hiebert said, "If behavioral change was the focus of the mission movement in the 19th century, and changed beliefs its focus in the 20th century, then transforming worldviews must be its central task in the 21st century."[1]

Colonizers and indigenous peoples of the South Pacific and Australasia

European missionaries first arrived to South Pacific people groups like the Australian Aborigines and New Zealand Māori in the 1700s. Many of these groups already had an understanding of a Father God/supreme God. Māoris in New Zealand and the Cook Islands believed in Io Matua Kore, the Father God who was above all other gods. A Māori priest named Toiroa actually had a vision in 1766, three years before Captain Cook would first arrive on New Zealand's shores. In his vision he saw light-skinned people wearing funny clothes, and he told his fellow Māori that these people would be bringing news of a good God named Tama-i-rorokutia (Son-who-was-killed) and that it would be very important to listen to them.[2]

Many Christians throughout the years have considered whether cultural adoption is needed to follow Christ. It is also the same question Paul addresses in Romans. Samuel Marsden, one of the first missionaries to the South Pacific, wrote this to his missions board back home: "It may be requisite to state that [indigenous] New Zealanders have derived no advantages hitherto either from commerce or the arts of civilization; and must, therefore, be in heathen darkness and ignorance. . . .They must not be considered by any means so favorably circumstanced for the reception of the gospel, as civilized nations are. . . .Since nothing in my opinion, can pave the way for the introduction of the Gospel but civilization."[3] For Marsden, the indigenous peoples needed to learn Western cultural norms in order to know God.

Churches initiated by indigenous people

Contrary to Marsden's belief, many of the indigenous peoples took what they had learned from the early missionaries and brought it to the rest of the islands. In New Zealand, there was a Māori-led church in the early 1800s with 5,000 Māori attending weekly, one of the largest on earth at that time. Missionaries in the Pacific Islands would arrive in new areas only to find out that the gospel had already arrived, already being carried by the local people. William Williams, a missionary at that time, stated, "A great work has been accomplished in which the hand of the Lord has been signally manifest. It has not been through the labor of your missionaries; for the word has only been preached by Native teachers. We had literally stood still to see the salvation of God."[4]

Sadly, European colonizers in Australia, New Zealand, and the South Pacific did not honor indigenous cultures. They would beat people for speaking their language. In some areas, children were taken away and placed with white families to ensure they would become "civilized." Some indigenous people groups have no desire to hear about Christianity because the ones who called themselves Christians were the very ones who abused and enslaved them. Just as in the marriage example, trust has been broken and an action needs to take place for trust to be rebuilt. Reconciliation is needed.

Reconciliation in the 21st century

So, how can we rebuild trust between peoples? An example of reconciliation happened in 2018 in Tauranga, New Zealand, between the Māori and the Anglican Church, which was the influential church in that area during the colonial period. A tract of land was given by the Māori to the English missionary Alfred Brown to establish a school. This school was so popular that Māori from hundreds of miles away would travel there to learn. When the Land Wars between Britain and the Māori developed in the mid-1800s, Brown was put in a tough place. Would he side with those to whom he came as a missionary, or give in to the pressures of his home nation? In the end, he sided with the British, and they confiscated the land that the mission had been using. Entire Māori tribes lost their homes and identity.[5]

In current-day Tauranga, a group of Christians formed a reconciliation group called Te Kohinga. One of the projects was this case of illegal land confiscation. They appealed to the New Zealand courts and the Anglican Church. Through years of research and talking with many of the descendants of the Māori tribes, they presented the criminality of what had happened. The Anglican Church apologized for their part in this conflict during an official ceremony in 2018. In response, the Māori Kaumatua (Chief), Puhirake Ihaka, said, "I thank you for your apology . . . .To me personally it brings some sense of relief, some sense of resolution and reconciliation, where in the latter clauses of your [apology] you say we have a relationship going forward."[6] What a profound statement! The whole point of reconciliation is for relationship to be healed. The Anglican Church has continued to restore relationship, working towards returning land to the Māori. That land transfer is scheduled to take place very soon. Across the world, similar situations are playing out. Many countries that were previously under the rule of another nation are beginning to use their own voice and seeing results.

Biblical vision: unity in diversity

At Pentecost, God could have completely reversed what He did at Babel and caused everyone to speak the same language. That He didn't speaks to His valuing of cultures and differences.

Reconciliation in missions is how we can take differing ideas and cultures and unite them under one heavenly Father. We can learn so much from each other, much in the same way we are strengthened in our differences in marriage. In Revelation 7 we see a picture described by John of "every tongue, tribe, and nation" worshipping God together and as one. May it be on earth as it is in heaven.

1. Paul Hiebert. *Transforming Worldviews.* (2008), p.11.
2. Judith Binney. "Myth and Explanation in the Ringatu Tradition," *The Journal of the Polynesian Society*, vol. 93, 4. (1984), p.353.
3. *Proceedings of the Church Missionary Society in Africa and the East.* (1806–1809), pp.961–963.
4. William Williams. *Christianity among the New Zealanders.* (1867), p.290.
5. Keith Newman. *Bible and Treaty.* (2010).
6. https://www.nzherald.co.nz/nz/news/article.cfm?c_id=1&objectid=12169112

About Dave Smith

Dave has served as a missionary in the South Pacific and Asia for nearly 10 years. During this time he's shared the love of Jesus in Australia, New Zealand, Vanuatu, Fiji, Singapore, Malaysia, Thailand, South Korea, Japan, Germany, and Mexico. David's passion is to lead intimate worship like his biblical namesake and to teach others about the love God has for each one of us. He lives with his wife, Alissa, and their three children in Tauranga, New Zealand.

30

Rest:
A Key to Fulfilling
the Great Commission

Shannon Graybill

Missions is such a big term. It encompasses so many different things: telling people about Jesus, discipleship, teaching, justice, and on and on. But there is an aspect of missions that I had to learn because it was a foreign concept to me: true Sabbath rest. When you are on the field in a traumatized nation, your life can seem to be wrapped up in other things 24/7. The effects of poverty don't cease to exist when it's 5 p.m. Working with traumatized people, I received calls at all hours of the day and night. You are always on call for whatever crisis or emergency might arise. There were days that seemed to go on for weeks with no break in sight.

When my grandfather passed away, someone asked me when I would take some time off to grieve and rest. My response was January, which was six months away. I definitely didn't think I had time; every month was booked with schools and programs and teachings, and then there were the people I was mentoring and discipling. Nope, rest would have to wait. Of course, January came and went with new months that filled with things that just had to be done. Meanwhile, my relationship with the Lord faltered, my reading the Word got pushed to the wayside, my friends didn't see me much, and even things that I loved to do, such as teaching, became an overwhelming task.

I had to recognize that while I was so busy caring for others, I had forgotten to take care of myself. In order for us to serve in the ways God wants us to, we have to make sure we ourselves are filled up in order to pour out. Jesus modeled this every time He went to spend time with the Father, away from the crowds. In Mark 1:35 we read, "Very early in the morning, while it was still dark, Jesus got up, left the house and went off to a solitary place, where he prayed." Of course, there were still needs to be tended, teachings to be shared, and conversations to be had, but He knew He needed renewal and refreshment—and He took it! He rested, He reflected, He connected with His Father. He knew when He was tired and weary and needed to be refueled. He did not get overwhelmed by all that were calling to Him, because He made sure He made rest a priority. He did not get overwhelmed to the point of exhaustion on a daily basis.

Rest doesn't just mean quiet communion with God. It's a part of it, but there are times when we just need some fun! I like to think that Jesus knew how to have fun. He celebrated with His friends. He had dinners and feasts with them. Who doesn't enjoy a table full of friends and delicious food?

I, unfortunately, learned this lesson too late! The danger of not taking time for rest and making it as much of a priority as helping others and managing crises, is that it can lead to burnout. This is a much deeper issue that can have far-reaching consequences. For me, not resting for years did lead to such an experience. Only when I sought wise counsel from others did I recognize and understand the immense need for rest and how not stopping was so detrimental to many aspects of my life. I actually needed to remove myself from the field and have an extended sabbatical to be able to get myself back into a healthy place again. Only then could I move forward with the gifts and call that God had placed on my heart. It was a hard lesson to learn, but I am so grateful for how God used the difficult situation and was with me no matter where in the world it took me, even back home for a season.

On the mission field, sometimes our relationship with God can be pushed to the back burner, because we know He's there with us. But that lack of intentional communion and rejuvenation can cause us to run on fumes rather than sustaining fuel. You can only go so far until you sputter to a stop. There is a reason God commanded a Sabbath rest! He knows exactly how big each of our tanks is and knows when we need refilling. When we stop our constant moving and relax, enjoy, and rejuvenate, we can find the rest we need to be able to move forward with Him.

About Shannon Graybill

Shannon, from Pennsylvania, served as a missionary in the United Kingdom, the Netherlands and then for many years in South Africa. She has led international missionary training schools and coordinated outreach teams in many nations.

31

Discovering
Family Missions

Wes Dudley

An important value in DOVE (the network of churches I am part of) is maintaining our global connections through short-term mission trips as well as networking with other international DOVE churches to see God's Kingdom advance. Over the years, many teams have been sent out and countless lives have been impacted; some even receive a call to go into full-time mission work. These opportunities exist for anyone that's willing to step out of their comfort zone, but what would it look like if one's entire family tagged along? One of the great inhibitors to people saying "yes" to a short-term trip is that they believe their children are too young or their family isn't ready to tackle something so intense. But, what if we looked at this from another angle?

Here are five reasons why you *should* pursue taking your spouse and children to another nation.

1. Seeking the Lord together as a family gives your children an opportunity to hear God speak

When our children are involved in the decision-making process for any type of family venture, it not only increases their faith, but they also can feel valued and even help take ownership for whatever next steps are involved.

2. Raising the money to participate provides an opportunity to see God's provision

Some of the greatest memories I have as a child is seeing God provide financially in a supernatural way for our family. Raising funds for a family mission trip gives children a chance to work alongside their siblings and parents toward a common goal, and it helps them see firsthand how God can move on people's hearts to give.

3. Taking your family with you on a short-term missions trip places each member in the position to do hard things

The Greek poet Homer once said, "A man who has been through bitter experiences and travelled far enjoys even his sufferings after a time." Taking your family with you on a short-term mission trip places each member in the position to do hard things. Whether it's just stepping out of everyday surroundings, or being pushed to the limit physically, emotionally, or mentally, stepping into a mission trip almost always helps shape one's perspective for the rest of their life, and can help remove the bubble wrap that we place around our kids.

4. Missions confronts our cultural assumptions and facilitates fresh perspectives

Tourism is a booming global business that many Americans have the privilege to experience. However, most mission trips don't provide you with the chance to merely be a tourist. Mission trips allow traveling to be done the right way, where you are typically forced to engage with the culture in ways that pull each member out of his or her comfort zone. Particularly with Western society, it can be quite healthy not only to travel to someplace unfamiliar, but also travel away from somewhere too familiar. Ben Sasse zeroes in on this topic in his book *The Vanishing American Adult*[1] when he says that most of our kids never have to do more than just show up for family vacation. Purposefully traveling into a brand new context or culture can help shatter those unhealthy paradigms.

5. Serving overseas produces relationships with those different from us and an increased sense of how God can use us

Do you want to see your children cultivate a love for other nations and build lasting relationships? Intentionally giving your family the chance to make new Kingdom connections on an international level will likely shape the course of their entire life. It not only gives them a greater picture of what God is doing in the world, but it allows them to see themselves being used by God in ways they may have never thought possible.

When God called Abram to leave his father's household and go to another land, God promised that "all the families of the earth shall be blessed" through his descendants (Genesis 12:3, ESV). There are so many ways that we see this blessing being poured out in our day, but there is something special that seems to happen when families seek to bless other families. Taking your entire family on a mission trip may really not be a feasible option depending on the current season, but don't allow your children's ages or a potentially daunting circumstance dictate how God may want to strengthen and build His Kingdom and change your family forever.

1 Ben Sasse. *The Vanishing American Adult: Our Coming-of-Age Crisis and how to Rebuild a Culture of Self-Reliance.* (2017).

About Wes Dudley

Wes has served as the missions director at DOVE Westgate Church since 2013 and has had the opportunity to participate with many short-term mission teams, as well as prepare and commission numerous long-term missionaries. He and his wife, Julianna, lived in Taiwan for over four years as missionary ESL teachers. Wes has a passion for networking with believers from other nations. He currently resides in Ephrata, Pennsylvania.

AFTERWORD

So, What Does This all Mean?

"For God so loved the world that he gave his one
and only Son, that whoever believes in him shall not
perish but have eternal life."
John 3:16

The task of the worldwide church is to proclaim and show that love of God to all peoples. The articles in this book remind us of the biblical basis of world missions but also point to the need for strategic focus, especially on the least-reached peoples of the world. We have learned of the sheer diversity of today's methods of, tools for, and approaches to missions. Indeed, all can be involved—men, women, children, families, those with special needs, businessmen and women, doctors, IT experts, Bible translators, teachers, and others. We are all needed to get the job done!

What can each one of us do?

Some can pray, for we know that proclaiming God's love for this world is spiritual work and that much is accomplished in prayer, for "the prayer of a righteous person is powerful and effective" (James 5:16). Others can give financial resources, for we also know that planting churches, sending people to the unreached, and works of compassionate service such as caring for orphans all require finances. And, of course, some of us can go—to bless, encourage, teach, work alongside local people in their desire to help their communities.

The authors of this book desire that in reading this compilation of articles, you will see some of the ways in which God works today. Moreover, we hope you will be inspired to participate in God's plan to bless all nations.

For information, or to discuss how God's mission might impact you, please contact us at dmi@dcfi.org. We would love to help you be part of God's plan for all peoples.

Dr. Peter Bunton, PhD.

Director, DOVE Mission International

STAY CONNECTED TO
DOVE Mission International

- Short-term teams
- Medical missions
- Long-term missions opportunities
- Six-month internships in other nations

www.dovemission.org

dmi@dcfi.org

Printed in Great Britain
by Amazon